D1333242

by Prue Coats

Illustrated by Will Garfit

The World Pheasant Association

Dedication

This book is dedicated to my husband Archie,
from whom I have learnt most, but not all of my cookery.
Tower Hill Farm, December 14th 1987.

British Library Cataloguing-in-Publication Data
Coats, Pru
  Prue's Country Kitchen
  1. Food: English Dishes – Recipes
  I. Title
  641.5942

Text copyright © Prudence E. Coats 1988.

Jacket and inside illustrations copyright © William Garfit 1988.

Acknowledgements
I should like to thank Colin Willock for kindly writing the foreword to this book and for his wise counsel and advice. Jean and Keith Howman for their help and enthusiasm, without which this book might never have got off the ground. Will Garfit who has done the illustrations, and who has managed to capture the flavour of our rather eccentric way of life. Shooting Times and Country Magazine for their kindness in allowing me to reprint several recipes. Likewise Countrysport for letting me use recipes printed by them. My thanks to various friends for parting with their culinary secrets. And last, but by no means least to my daughter Lucy who has had the unenviable task of editing this book.

P.E.C.

First published in Great Britain in 1988 by

The World Pheasant Association
Ashmere

ISBN 1-871060-01-X
Printed and bound in Great Britain by A. Wheaton & Co Ltd.
Designed by Wheaton Publishers
All rights reserved

Contents

Foreword

By Colin Willock

Some thirty years ago, when I was editing the national magazine 'Lilliput' and writing for 'Farmers Weekly', Jack Hargreaves (of 'Out of Town' television fame, who was then my managing editor at Hulton Press) told me that there was a chap in Hampshire who made his living by shooting wood pigeons, name of Archie Coats. Jack and I were constantly seeding each other with ideas. It was I who introduced him to wildfowling. In return he was responsible, through this casual piece of information, for introducing me to Archie and Prue Coats. He did me many good turns but this was undoubtedly the best of them.

I remember that I sent a journalist on the staff of 'Lilliput', Malcolm Monteith, to investigate the Coats situation. By some strange coincidence about half of the editorial staff of 'Lilliput' were keen shooting or fishing men: it is a coincidence, incidentally, that has followed me through most of my working life, but let that pass.

Malcolm wrote an excellent piece about the mysterious Coats which duly appeared in a Hulton Press sister publication, 'Farmers Weekly'. Malcolm was so impressed with the Coats way of life that he suggested that I should perhaps go and see for myself. A few weeks after the publication of the article, which I recall was headlined 'Thirteen Thousand Pigeons a Year', I found myself at Tower Hill Farm, Dummer, in the county of Hampshire receiving the sort of welcome for which Chez Coats has since become famous.

I sensed at once that if Coats was the ultimate Master in one field of activity, then Mrs Coats was the Supreme Mistress of another. In short, she cooked superbly and variously some of the 13,000 woodies that fell to Archie's gun each year. As she says in this book, she was never of the 'Pigeon Pie' persuasion. Woodies provided excellent protein which was capable of being turned into pâtés and terrines, salmis and escalopes, casseroles and sautés of infinite variety, flavour and sophistication. If you do not believe that the wood pigeon, in the right kitchen, is a cordon bleu bird, then try some of the recipes in this book. If you own or have access to a fisherman's hot smoker, do not fail to make Prue Coats' smoked pigeon pâté. But I am allowing myself to be swept ahead on a flood tide of gastronomic enthusiasm. There are many other recipes in this book that do not concern pigeons.

After our first meeting I was invited fairly regularly to go pigeon shooting with the Master. In fact, all that I now know about that difficult and fascinating craft I learned at the Master's feet. At that time Coats and the Hampshire pigeons were at their peak.

In her introduction, Prue has described how Archie came to be a professional pigeon shooter. I believe she has left out one important chapter in the story. Archie, of course, had shot since a boy. But it was as a wartime instructor at Sandhurst, at the end of the war, that the pigeon potential of Hampshire struck him with the force of a Jerry 88 millimetre air-burst. At week ends he spent his leave from Sandhurst shooting pigeons and paying his hotel bills by selling the slain. In those days pigeons were more valuable, as an addition to rations, than at any time before or since.

It may seem strange to some readers that after the war he persuaded a large Hampshire land-owner to retain him simply to keep the pigeons off their crops. But the fact was that in those days Hampshire, Wiltshire and Berkshire were infested with wood pigeons and stock doves (the latter are now protected though for what reason, heaven knows). Moreover, those naturally wiley birds were then fairly unsophisticated about such subterfuges as decoys.

A flock of one thousand pigeons could, and did, decimate a crop within days if not forcibly dissuaded. The field had then to be sown again with loss of time, labour and revenue. To prevent this, Coats was on call to his sponsors, seven days a week if necessary. It often was necessary. A great many pigeons were shot – he was then averaging about 70 per cent kills. Perhaps more important, thousands more were kept away from valuable crops just when they were most vulnerable.

At this time I was learning the trade with the Master. At first I found it extremely intimidating to have Coats breathing down my neck in a bale hide, calling me, in a tone that a deaf woodie could hear a mile away, all kinds of an inadequate shot, at least I *think* that was the word, or one of the words, he used.

As I got to know him better I realised that Archie Coats was the original paper tiger. To use another zoological comparison, he might huff and he might puff but he would never blow your hide down. He is far too kind a man to do any real damage to your self-esteem. By the time I could more or less guarantee to kill one wood pigeon for three cartridges, I was awarded the accolade of being Twelfth Man in his Third Eleven. When I eventually graduated to a consistent two-to-one or slightly better ratio, I was put on the reserve list for the Coats 'A' Team. It was better than getting your first eleven colours at Prep school.

I have shared many of the best moments at Tower Hill with Will Garfit whose delightful drawings illustrate this book. Will, who is one of the foremost landscape artists of the day, regards Archie as his sporting godfather. He first went pigeon shooting with him when he was still at art school. I would say that as an all-round shot Will Garfit is opening batsman for the Coats First Eleven.

Will understands Archie possibly better than anyone save Prue. He knows, for instance, that the great man does not feel that all is right with his world unless something is going wrong. Will often stays at Tower Hill the night before the famous ten acres is to be shot. His role is to get up before light and tap in the neighbouring farmer's hedges, with the neighbouring farmers' approval it must be added, so that every pheasant within half a mile is persuaded to return to the Coats' policies where they have probably been lovingly reared, anyway.

One morning Will returned from his dawn patrol to find that everything was going perfectly to plan. Too perfectly! The Master had nothing to huff and puff about. So, Will very sensibly went outside in the farmyard and let down one of the tyres of Coat's Land Rover. When he discovered the flat tyre Coats was immediately restored to form. Something had gone wrong. Here was something he could happily swear about. From then on all was sweetness and light and all went well.

WIll and I, together with other regular pigeon shooting friends, share another affectionate joke about Archie. He is frequently known in the environs of Dummer by his former military rank – The Major. Often when we have rung him as to what time to report for pigeon duty the following day the telephone wire has come close to burning up with a diabtribe that goes something like this: 'They were on the peas in thousands two days ago. There was absolutely sweet f.a. there yesterday. I don't know where they've all gone. Probably into the next county. . . . '

Now one waits for the famous pay-off line. 'My dear boy, come if you like, but I tell you it's a *Major Disaster*.' Inevitably, then, Archie is sometimes referred to by his close friends as Major Disaster. By the way, it seldom is. He never is!

Regular attendance at Tower Hill Farm has brought other inestimable benefits. Sometimes I was ordered to be there for breakfast – 'pigeons start feeding early, my boy, these dark winter mornings.' Often in summer we didn't get back from the field of battle until it was nearly dark – 'Sometimes they don't really switch on until five or six in the evening.' Early start or late finish, it meant a chance to sample Mrs Coat's culinary skills. It was soon clear that many of the dishes she devised were designed to complement the by no means normal life-style and irregular hours of a professional pigeon shooter (not to mention gastronome) and the friends who accompanied him at his work.

Without doubt, Prue's *tour de force* is the lunch that follows the two annual shoots on the Coats estate. These are known as Tower Hill One and Tower Hill Two. She has touched upon these great sporting events in this book. I hope she will not mind if once again I fill in a few gaps.

The Tower Hill shoots are remarkable for a number of things, but most of all for the gastronomic events that follows the hour-and-a-half taken to complete a beating manoeuvre that is as hallowed a ritual as the Trooping of the Colour. Incidentally it involves almost as many orders (and counter-orders) given by the Master and woe betide any wife who forgets to dress by the right in the beating line or fails to troop her colour or at least wave her fertiliser bag on a stick at the moment a pheasant gets airborne.

The bag is often between forty and sixty pheasants and a few 'various' – not bad for ten acres, quite a large portion of which is covered by a minature Black Forest of over-grown Christmas trees. It goes without saying that since most of the invited guns belong either to the Coats First or Second Elevens, not many pheasants escape. The buffet lunch that follows is wondrous, especially the pâtés and terrines. But then you can prove this for yourself since all the dishes offered to guns, wives and girlfriends at Tower Hill One and Two appear in these pages.

And talking of pages, early on in our friendship I discovered that Archie Coats, among his many other talents, has that rare and fortunate gift of being a natural writer. He had already written a good many articles about his unique way of earning a living. His words flowed because he wrote much as he talked (with asterisks deleted). It wasn't too hard to persuade him that he should write a book.

In fact he wrote two, 'Pigeon Shooting' and 'The Amateur Keeper'. The former has become a shooting classic and the second is much in demand by those who run their own shoots and are lucky enough to have a copy.

For years, many of her friends, and not least her husband, tried to persuade Prue Coats that she should follow Archie's example and pass on the culinary knowledge that was uniquely hers.

It took a good deal of arm-twisting. Reasonably enough she protested that there were far too many cookery books already; that to make any sort of dent in the market any new addition to the over-stocked shelves just had to have something different about it.

My reply was: 'Can you think of anything more different than the kind of life you and Archie live and the recipes you have invented to make the most of the game and country produce under which Tower Hill Farm has at times been practically buried?' Reluctantly she admitted that she couldn't, though rightly insisted that – if she agreed to write such a book – many of the recipes must be practical ones of her own invention for the majority of cooks who don't spend their lives in a cloud of game and pigeon feathers.

I know that, unlike Archie, Prue did not find that writing came easily. But then many of the best writers don't! With a little help from her friends, and no end of encouragement from her spouse, she has produced a unique cookery book in which recipes and anecdotes alike flow as smoothly off the page as treacle off a warm spoon.

There were, I believe, two other factors that, if you will forgive the expression, egged her on. One, she acquired a word processor and fell in love with it. Two, her daughter Lucy is a successful publisher's editor and thus was able to offer not only encouragement but professional advice.

The Coats' married partnership is a remarkable one. These days Archie still shoots pigeons two or three days a week and more if called upon. I use the word 'still' not in deference to advancing years but because both the Master's hips have packed up and won't accept the artificial joints that work so well for most hip sufferers. He is therefore on crutches and, at times, only just on crutches.

Every time he goes pigeon shooting, therefore, and when there isn't a friend to assist, which is most of the time, Prue goes out with him, puts him in his hide, and retrieves him at the end of the day.

How you find time to write a cookery book when you're doing all that, I just don't know. What I do know is that she did it.

MENU

Duck Liver Pâté with Brandy & Truffles
Grouse Pâté with Whisky & Juniper berries
Partridge Liver Pâté with Paprika
Smoked Pigeon Pâté with Vermouth
Trout Pâté with Almonds
Terrine of Pigeon with Sloe Gin
Terrine of Mallard with Madeira

Spinach Mousse with cheese & hard boiled egg

Chicory, Orange & Juniper Salad
Celeriac Remoulade
Fennel in Pernod Sauce
Radiccio & Lettuce

Oxtail Stew
Shootable Stag or Devilled Kidneys

Chocy Pots
Elderberry Mousse
Tangerine Sorbet

Cheese & Biscuits — Coffee

17.X.87

A Ten Acre Shoot, Luncheon Menu

Introduction

This book has happened as a result of our rather unusual life-style. About six months after we were married Archie came in one day and said he didn't think he could bear to go on living in London and working in an office for the rest of his life. So he asked me what I thought of the idea of him becoming a professional wood pigeon shooter. After some soul-searching I agreed, and so we came to Hampshire as that was where the pigeons were. Little did I know what this would all lead to.

As he brought in piles of pigeons, so we had to market them, and of course one way to do this was to interest people in how to cook them, and to wean them away from the 'Pigeon Pie' mentality. The second side of our activities came about through a friend of ours who was Managing Director of the Savoy Hotel. He came to shoot pigeons, and for supper we gave him Fraises des Bois (cultivated wild strawberries) which I had grown from a packet of seed bought on holiday in France. He was so entranced that he persuaded us to grow them for the Savoy Group. I sowed ten packets of seed and they all germinated so I ordered a hundred pots and one bag of compost, but we ended up with six-and-a-half thousand pots and a ton of compost and the start of a thriving business for twenty odd years. In order to keep my pickers on the payroll in the winter months Archie decided to go into the 'oven-ready' game business. Not all the birds you buy off the shoot are perfect so I was always being landed with what my 'Ladies' call 'dodgies' or 'oldies'. This led to inventing new recipes to use them up, in particular pâtés and terrines, which is why there are so many of those in this book.

Yet another of our early ventures was Christmas trees, but one year a major London store imported a million plastic trees, so ours became unsaleable. The net result of this was that Archie decided to make the ground into a mini shoot and thus was born the 'Ten Acre Shoot' so aptly described by our friend Colin Willock, who writes under the guise of 'Town Gun' in the *Shooting Times*, and who has kindly written the foreword to this book. You can hardly ask people to shoot for two hours so this is how it came about that after 'stopping', beating, plunging through head high nettles, waving flags and being bawled at I had to produce a really gastronomic lunch for between twenty-five and thirty people.

Life at Tower Hill is never dull. We have people to stay nearly every weekend and friends often drop in, so I have to be ready to produce a 4-star meal at pretty short notice. This is why I am a great believer in using your imagination – if you haven't got a particular ingredient, then never be afraid to use something else. Don't hesitate to use a short cut if you are in a hurry. It is fun to try the classic way once and then you know how it is done and what is involved. For example people get all hot under the collar about making clear consommé. I agree that the process is time consuming, but it does look nice. Frankly, though the pundits will probably disagree, the taste is exactly the same as it was before you went to all the trouble of wasting egg whites and spending hours whisking.

I don't like too much garnish or over decoration. The French have got it down to a fine art. You may go to any little country restaurant and the presentation will be simple. Just a sprig of cress, two or three slices of orange or lemon, a handful of olives, but nothing to distract your eye from the dish you are about to eat. Decoration should merely enhance the food and make it seem more delectable.

My cookery has been entirely self-taught. At the beginning of the war my mother could hardly boil an egg, so I did not inherit any skills from her. Luckily I am by nature greedy and really enjoy food and trying out new recipes, or endeavouring to copy something I have tasted. Archie has taught me a great deal as he is a very good cook himself. He, in fact learnt at the great Escoffier's school in Paris before the war, where he gained a proficiency certificate in meat and sauces. You may ask why a young man of twenty should have been attending a cookery school. His explanation is that he could only see his current girl friend in the evening, at the said school, where she was taking a cookery course. Whether this is true or not I shall never know, but that is his story and he has stuck to it for thirty-five years! Luckily our daughter, Lucy, is also a good cook and greedy to boot, so she and Archie are very severe critics – if one of my new recipes passes muster with them I am pretty sure I am onto a winner.

Finally, this is, above all a country cookery book and many of the recipes contain herbs and ingredients you may not think are available if you live in a town. However, nowadays most garden centres have a good selection of herbs in pots and you can always grow one or two in a window box. Game is nearly always available in season in the bigger supermarkets. If not, don't be afraid to ask your butcher, he can nearly always get what you want from the market, and in the country some farm shops sell game, so keep a look out when you are away for the weekend.

This book is geared to the busy or working woman who may not have time to cook elaborate meals. Some of the recipes are quickies for just two of you, and some are more advanced, for dinner parties. I find it very annoying to scrabble through several cookery books for specialized recipes, such as sloe gin, so I have tried to include all the particular things that I use and that we, as a family like. Everything has been tried and tested by Archie, Lucy and friends, and I can only say that they seem to come back for more.

Cook's Equipment

Now I come to my personal 'Batterie de Cuisine'. Saucepans are very much a matter of individual taste, but if you are starting from scratch, do spend as much as you can afford on them as they should last you a lifetime. I have three good quality stainless steel saucepans and they are as good as new, although they are at least thirty years old. I also have a set of Le Creuset cast iron saucepans and a milk saucepan coated in Castoflon. This is quite excellent. Food really does not stick to it and you can use metal spoons and whisks and they do not leave scratches. If you have weak wrists you will find that cast iron saucepans are heavy to lift and pour from. In that case stainless steel would be better. Thick cast iron frying pans, large, medium and small are essential for sautéeing, but they must be cherished after the initial 'proving' has taken place. By this I mean that you heat the pan over a low heat, pour in some oil and continue to heat until the oil smokes. Then pour it away and rub with kitchen paper. You should do this every time after use and in the end your pans will be become virtually non-stick.

A cast iron enamelled casserole is a must, and likewise one in earthenware – the size dictated by your family requirements. Two or three shallow earthenware dishes in different sizes are useful, plus one square or oblong shape which is handy if you cook lasagne.

All these things are very much a matter of taste and even after thirty-five years I am still adding and discarding.

Don't spare expense on knives and don't buy just because they look nice. *Do* hold them and see if they feel comfortable. My own knives comprise:-

1 large 8″ (20cm) Cook's knife. This should be so finely balanced that it virtually chops
things of its own volition.
1 smaller Cook's knife 7″ (17½cm)
1 medium boning knife 5″ (12½cm)
2 or 3 thin tapered knives 5″ (12½cm) 4½″ (11½cm) 4″ (10cm)
1 small pointed knife 3″ (7½cm)

Another essential is a good quality knife sharpener. Mine is made by Kitchen Devil and is called Professional Choice. You should also have a proper butcher's steel with a good guard on the handle, to prevent the knife slipping and cutting you as you stroke the blade down the steel towards you. If you can learn to use

W.G.

one of these it will make your life much easier, as there is nothing more frustrating than trying to carve or cut up things with a blunt knife. I like to keep my knives in one of those wooden knife blocks which can always be at hand. Those magnetic knife racks are fine for small knives, but I always found I was knocking them off. You should also have:-

    1 large balloon whisk

    1 medium whisk

    2 tiny balloon whisks (they come 2 together on a card, one with a long and one with a short, handle). Absolutely invaluable for making small quantities of salad dressing and mayonnaise.

Do spend a little money and invest in a pair of old fashioned balance scales with a set of imperial and metric weights. This makes life easier when you are trying to adapt recipes.

You can't have enough bowls, I have:-

    3 large pyrex bowls

    2 medium bowls about 8″ (20cm)

    2 Elizabeth David earthenware bowls with a brown rim and pouring lip. Make sure at least one of your bowls fits over a saucepan so that you can use it for Sauce Bearnaise *p.31*, or anything which needs cooking over hot water, in other words a 'bain marie'.

    4×4″ and 5″ (10cm and 12 ½cm) for making small quantities of things in and for keeping small quantities in the fridge.

Now I come to the electrical gadget department, and absolutely top of my list comes my Magimix food processor. Next comes the pair of small electric hand beaters. I find them quite sufficient for my cake making, but if you make a lot of cakes then I suppose a Kenwood Chef or the like is the answer. I also have two other electrical gadgets, neither of which is essential, but both make life easier, a herb chopper and a citrus juicer.

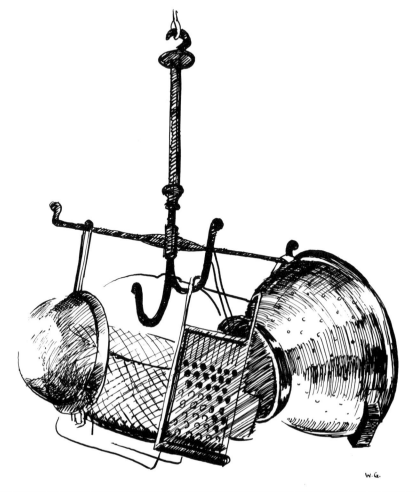

W.G.

12

Finally I come to the store cupboard, which of course includes the freezer nowadays. I shall only list the extras which I find useful.

Green peppercorns
Green peppercorn purée
Coarse and Fine sea salt. These are natural and free from any artificial preservative and I never use anything else.
Chicken Seasoning
Lamb Seasoning
Whole nutmegs
Ground cloves
Mace
Ground ginger
Fresh root ginger
Minced or powdered garlic for when you run out of fresh garlic
Cinnamon sticks
Vanilla pods
Vanilla sugar – caster sugar in

a screwtop jar with a vanilla pod stuck in the middle
Vanilla rice – short grain pudding rice as above
Mixed dried herbs
Best quality olive oil
Sunflower oil. Best for frying – not so smelly
Wine vinegar
Dijon Mustard
Packet of undyed breadcrumbs, known in France as chapelure, (or make them yourself)
Runny honey
Redcurrant jelly
Hot curry paste
Hot curry powder
Potato flour

Other suggestions for your store cupboard:-

Tins of tuna fish and a jar of Hellman's mayonnaise for *Peta's Tuna Fish Salad p.87.* Small tinned button mushrooms and tinned Italian tomatoes for *Sante's Tagliatelle p.103* and concentrated Tomato purée for *Lasagne p.102.* You should have some bacon and cheese in the fridge and one or two bags of cream and pots of potted shrimps and frozen prawns in the freezer. Of course the list is endless, but I think these suggestions are helpful, especially for unexpected guests.

Here are a few explanations of some of the cooking terms:
'Bain Marie' = a bowl or container which is placed over hot water and used to cook sauces etc in.
Dredging = to coat something in flour or other ingredient
Reduce/reduction = reduce quantity of liquid by fast boiling
Shiver = simmer

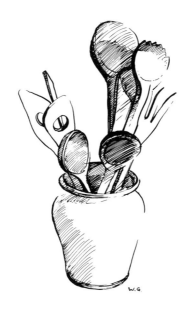

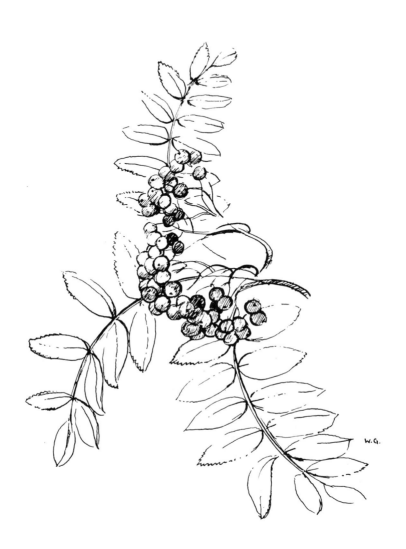

Herbs, Herb Vinegars Oils & Condiments

We love herbs, and being lucky enough to live in the country have enough space to grow them. But if you live in a town even a pot or two make all the difference and if you can manage a window box of say, thyme, parsley, chives and marjoram, all the better. I never dry herbs nowadays, it is so much easier to freeze them. Pick herbs on a dry sunny day when they will be at their most aromatic. Freeze on the stalk on trays, and when stiff you can pull the leaves off quite easily. Store in firmly sealed plastic boxes or tubs, label clearly on the lid and put in your freezer basket where they will be easily accessible. Another method is to freeze them whole in large plastic bags, then scrunch them up and transfer to the plastic container.

The following are what I grow.

Basil	Annual. Likes lots of sun. Oval pointed leaves, essential ingredient in some of my pâtés, in pasta sauces, tomato salad, tomato soup, lasagne and many other dishes. Freeze.
Chervil	Annual. Parsley-like leaves with a slightly aniseed flavour. Makes a delicious soup, use also with fish or eggs as a change from fennel. Freeze.
Chives	Perennial. Onion family. Easily grown in a pot. If cherished and watered with Baby Bio will become luxuriant. All kinds of uses, especially in salads, mayonnaise, and as a garnish. Freeze, but best fresh.
Coriander	Annual. Parsley-like plant. Can be grown in a pot. Leaves for use in salads, soups and the ripe seeds, crushed and used in curries and Greek and Turkish dishes. Freeze leaves, dry seeds.
Dill	Annual. Feathery leaves. An essential ingredient of Gravadlax. Also good in fish pâtés. Freeze.
Fennel	Annual. Tall feathery spikes. Use in fish dishes, but stronger than dill. Freeze.
Horseradish	Perennial. Very strong root, especially in winter. Grate and make sauce for beef and smoked trout. Must be used fresh as loses potency when dried or bottled.
Marjoram	Perennial. Pretty round-leaved plant. Goes well with beans and in all kinds of meat casseroles.
Mint	Perennial. Best grown in a pot or container as it spreads like mad. Try and get Apple Mint, it has a more delicate flavour. Freezes well and has a variety of uses in dishes both savoury and sweet.
Parsley	Biennial. Takes well to pot life providing you don't neglect it and forget to water. Universally known and has a wide range of uses.
Rosemary	Perennial shrub. Pointed spiky leaves with blue flowers. Aromatic and decorative. Use with lamb and with some Italian dishes. Dry – don't freeze.

Sage	Perennial shrub. Very strong grey pointed leaves. Use sparingly except with calves liver. Not really suitable for towndwellers unless you have a garden when it makes a nice grey foliage plant. If no garden pinch some leaves from a friend and freeze. One of the few herbs that dries well.
Sorrel	Perennial. Same family as the dock. Lemony flavour. Delicious as soup and in sauces. You really need a row of about 6 plants, but one plant in an 8″ (20cm) pot would be sufficient to flavour a sauce. Use fresh.
Tarragon	Perennial. Lance-shaped leaves growing in tall spires. Essential for Sauce Bearnaise, Poulet a l'Estragon, in salads, mayonnaise and with mushrooms. Freeze.
Thyme	Perennial. Grows well in a pot. Very strong and aromatic. Use in stews, pâtés, terrines, pasta sauces, lasagne. Another herb to dry and not freeze.

This is not a comprehensive list of herbs, just my special favourites. Chopped up fresh they can be used to flavour either vinegars or oils which I use to make my special salad dressings.

HERB VINEGARS AND OILS

TARRAGON VINEGAR

2 pints (1 litre) white wine vinegar
1 pint (575ml) fresh tarragon leaves picked on a dry, sunny day.

Beg a plastic sweet jar from your local shop, but make sure it hasn't been used for aniseed balls! Wash it out well, put in the tarragon leaves and crush them with a wooden spoon. Pour on the vinegar, screw on the top and leave in a dark cool cupboard for one month. Then strain into clean sterlised bottles, insert a branch of tarragon and screw on the caps.

MIXED HERB VINEGAR

2 pints (1 litre) red wine vinegar
1 tablespoon each of chopped parsley, chives, tarragon, marjoram and thyme.

Follow the same method as above.
You can make herb vinegar of any other herbs such as chervil, fennel, or dill for use sparingly in fish dishes.
You could halve or quarter the quantities.

GARLIC VINEGAR

1 pint (575ml) red wine vinegar
12 cloves garlic

Crush the garlic, boil the vinegar and pour over. Leave for one month, strain and bottle.

CHILLIE VINEGAR

1 pint red wine vinegar
1 oz (25g) dried red chillies

Cut the chillies up with a pair of scissors. Bring the vinegar to the boil, pour onto the chillies and bottle. Strain as you use.

CHILLIE SHERRY

This, according to a naval friend who was once Flag Lieutenant to an Admiral, was mandatory in the wardroom. He was not alone amongst our naval friends with this predilection so I suppose it helped to enliven boring food on board ship.

1 small tonic water bottle full of sherry
3 dried red chillies

Insert the chillies into the bottle of sherry, leave for a few days and use very sparingly in soup. It gets stronger with age, so you can top it up with more sherry until it starts to lose its potency.

Herb flavoured oils are delicious in salads or used when you grill chops or steak. But do use the very finest olive oil and only make a small quantity as once opened they should be refrigerated and used as soon as possible.

GARLIC OIL

8 fl oz (250ml) best olive oil
6 unskinned cloves of garlic

Wash and sterilize a small tonic water bottle, put in the cloves of garlic and fill up with olive oil. Stopper and leave for two weeks. Use as soon as possible after opening.

MIXED HERB OIL

8 fl oz (250 ml) best olive oil
1 sprig each of thyme, marjoram and rosemary
3 bayleaves

Follow above procedure.

BLACK OLIVES IN HERBS, GARLIC & OIL

Fill a screwtop jar with best quality ripe black olives. They should look wrinkled and feel soft when you pinch them. You will find them at any good delicatessen. Greek or Italian ones are best, the Spanish variety tend to be rather hard. As you fill the jar keep sprinkling in Herbes de Provence and chopped garlic, then pour in best quality olive oil. Store in a dark cupboard for at least one month. Use as required in salads, or with drinks as a snack.

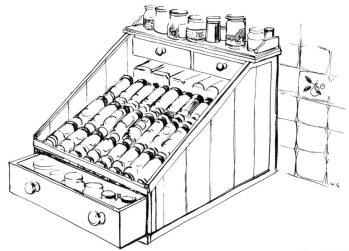

ARCHIE'S MUSTARD

Or The Boss's own blend. When making this he looks like a wizard concocting a potent spell or potion, and it is certainly strong. His theory is that you should marry the hot Colman's mustard powder with one dark, one light and one 'grainy' mustard. As I always have different continental mustards in the cupboard it was difficult to standardize the product so that we could actually write down ingredients which were readily available. I finally came up with the following which, I am pleased to say, has passed muster.

8 tablespoons Colman's dry mustard powder
1 small pot (90g) Colman's French Mustard (dark)
1 small pot (90g) Colman's Dijon Mustard (light, mild)
½ pot (45g) Colman's Whole Grain Mustard

1 dessertspoon Schwartz Minced Garlic or garlic powder
1 dessertspoon Mixed Herbs
2 tablespoons sugar

Place all the dry ingredients in a bowl and mix together, then add the mustards and beat well with electric hand beaters. Spoon into a screw top jar or empty stoneware Moutarde de Meaux jar and stopper tightly. Leave for 24 hours and then taste. If it is too vinegary add some more sugar.

Archie is always complaining that there is never any left for him after we've had guests, but we tell him that he should be pleased that so many of his friends like it. He also likes to eat it with toast and marmalade – try it and see!

ARCHIE'S PEPPER OR CONDIMENT

Another of Archie's 'specials'. We used to use a lot of Lawry's Seasoned Pepper as the main ingredient, but alas this is no longer readily available, so that is why the following mixture was dreamed up.

2 teaspoons ground black peppercorns
2 teaspoons ground white peppercorns
1 teaspoon ground green peppercorns
½ teaspoon ground allspice
1 teaspoon lemon pepper
1 teaspoon garlic powder or garlic pepper
1 ½ teaspoons fine sea salt
¼ teaspoon cayenne pepper

Place everything in an empty seasoning jar with a screw top and perforated inner lid. Use a spoon to mix, replace both lids, screw up tightly and shake well.

Soups

Stock is a great standby for all sorts of recipes, and if you have a deep freeze you need never be short. Whenever we have chicken, game or pigeon, the carcasses go straight into the pressure cooker, where they brew for at least 2 hours with the usual carrot, onion, celery stalk, salt, pepper and pinch of mixed herbs. Lucy is fanatic about this and gets furious with me if I am in an idle mood and surreptitiously try and throw away even a few bones before making them into stock. Once I have made the stock I take off the saucepan lid and boil rapidly and reduce by half. This makes it more concentrated and saves space in the freezer. If you get your milk in cartons, wash them out and use them as containers for your stock and soup in the freezer. It saves both money and space.

The three most common ways of thickening soup are:

1. *Potato.* Added as an ingredient when cooking vegetable soup will make it thicker when blended.
2. *Beurre Manié.* Equal quantities of butter and flour, kneaded or processed, then dropped bit by bit into boiling soup whisking continuously until it is thick enough.
3. *Potato Flour* or *Cornflour.* Mix the required quantity, (usually 1-2 heaped teaspoons) in a little cold liquid then add to the boiling soup or stew. Stir to remove lumps and cook for a few minutes.

Good home-made soup can be a meal in itself, and if you have a food processor or liquidizer it takes just seconds to whizz something up. One of the best soups I ever made contained all the left-overs from the fridge, including a wedge of apple pie! Of course these are 'once onlys' and this is where your imagination comes in. All vegetable soups should have sugar as part of the seasoning, as it sets off the flavour. You will find that many of my recipes contain something sweet in the way of honey or jelly. This has been dinned into me over the years by Archie who firmly believes in the Chinese precept of 'sweet and sour', or 'Yin and Yang', which is to say the marriage of opposites to make a harmonious whole. Strangers seeing Archie eat vegetable soup gaze in horror at the amount of sugar he puts in. I think he rather overdoes it but certainly some sweetness does improve most soups.

BORTSCH

This is the 'real McCoy' and the recipe was given to me by the beautiful Russian-born wife of a cousin. It is a labour of love to make it and the accompanying Pirozhki, but it is well worth all the trouble.

Marrowbone Stock

1 marrowbone cut in pieces by the butcher
(approx 1 ½ lbs – 675 g)
1 large carrot
1 large onion
1 stalk celery
1 leek
1 bayleaf
6 peppercorns
bouquet garni (bunch consisting of 1 stalk
parsley, 1 sprig thyme, 1 sprig marjoram) or,
½ teaspoon mixed herbs
½ lemon
½ teaspoon salt
4 pints (2 litres) water

Put all these ingredients into a large saucepan and cover tightly. Bring slowly to the boil and simmer for 3 to 4 hours. Strain through a colander over which you have laid a clean tea towel. Blot off the fat with squares of kitchen paper.

The Bortsch Soup

2 pints (1 litre) marrowbone stock or 2 tins consommé made up to this amount, if you are feeling lazy and can't be bothered to make the marrowbone stock.

1 lb (450g) peeled, grated raw beetroot for initial cooking and flavouring.

8 oz (225g) peeled raw beetroot, finely grated then processed in the Magimix for serving.

1 dessertspoon concentrated tomato purée
1 beef stock cube
1 squeeze lemon juice
1 dash Worcester Sauce
1 dessertspoon sugar
salt and pepper to taste   **Serves 6-8**

Put the marrowbone stock (or tinned consommé) into a saucepan, add the 1lb (450g) grated beetroot, bring to the boil and simmer until the beetroot is drained of colour. Strain into another saucepan and add the 8oz (225g) of finely grated and processed beetroot, tomato purée, stock cube (if necessary – it shouldn't be), lemon juice, Worcester Sauce, sugar, salt and pepper and heat through. Serve with Pirozhki (recipe below).

Pirozhki

8 oz (225g) bought puff pastry
8 oz (225g) finely ground lean mince
1 teaspoon finely chopped shallot
¼ clove garlic, crushed
1 pinch mixed herbs
1 teaspoon concentrated tomato purée
1 dash Worcester Sauce
1 teaspoon sunflower oil
salt and ground black pepper

Heat the oil in a small pan until smoking. Put in the mince and chopped shallot and brown lightly. Turn down the heat and add all the other ingredients. Cover tightly and cook over a very low heat for 1½ hours or until tender. Moisten with a little stock if it begins to look dry. Let it get quite cold.

Roll out the pastry until it is very thin and cut into 2″ (5cm) squares or rounds and place a teaspoon of mince in the centre of each. Moisten the edges and press together. Brush with egg yolk and milk and place in a preheated oven at 400°F 200°C Gas Mark 6 for 8-10 minutes or until they look golden and puffed up. Serve with the Bortsch.

You can also serve the Bortsch as a consommé without the addition of the grated/processed beetroot and with a swirl of cream or cream and lemon juice. In the summer you can serve it en gelée (it should set on its own if you make it with the marrowbone stock) and decorate each cup with a blob of whipped cream and chives. By the way, the reason I gave such strange instructions for the beetroot to be served in the soup was that when I followed Tania's directions to grate the beetroot, when we came to eat it the process was rather like trying to eat spaghetti and particularly messy as the beetroot juice dripped all down our chins. So I got round the problem by first grating and then processing with the cutting blade of the Magimix. Don't freeze.

BROAD BEAN SOUP

This is a great way of using up the more elderly broad beans which have developed a 'leather overcoat'.

1lb (450g) shelled fresh or frozen broad beans
1 pint (575ml) water or chicken stock
½ chicken stock cube (optional)
1 dessertspoon sugar
1 good pinch marjoram or basil
salt and ground black pepper
cream   **Serves 4-6**

Simmer the broad beans in water or stock with all the other ingredients except the cream until tender. Liquidize until smooth, thin with milk if too stodgy. Adjust seasoning and serve with a blob of cream and a sprig of marjoram or basil in each soup cup. In summer serve ice cold. Freezes well.

CARROT SOUP

Delicious either hot or cold. It can be thick and filling for a cold winter's day or smoother and more delicate for a dinner party, or chilled in summer.

8 oz (225g) carrots
2 oz (50g) peeled onion
2 oz (50g) peeled potato
1 heaped teaspoon sugar
1 pint (575ml) water or chicken stock

1 heaped teaspoon chopped Parsley or Mint
salt and ground black pepper to taste
cream (optional)   Serves 2-4

Slice the carrots, chop the onion and potato roughly and put into a saucepan with the butter. Place over a low heat and stir until coated with the butter. Cover and shake occasionally to prevent sticking. When the vegetables begin to look transparent add the water or stock and simmer until tender, about 15 minutes. Place in blender and process until smooth. Serve hot with croutons. If you are making the summer version, omit the potato and thicken with 1 heaped teaspoon potato flour or cornflour mixed with a little milk. Serve chilled and garnished with a blob of cream and some chopped mint or parsley in each soup cup. Freezes well.

LENTIL SOUP

This is almost a meal in itself and if possible should be made with some of the water in which you have cooked gammon. Failing this, if you have a good pork butcher or pie shop get them to let you have some kind of ham bone or the little bones which they cut out of a side of bacon.

8 oz (225g) green lentils
8 oz (225g) brown lentils
8 oz (225g) red lentils
1 large onion trimmed but unpeeled and stuck with cloves
1 ham bone or bacon bones
2 slices smoked streaky bacon finely chopped

1 clove garlic
2 pints (1 litre) water or 1 pint (575ml) water and 1 pint (575ml) ham stock
1 dessertspoon demerara sugar
salt and freshly ground black pepper
                    Serves 6-8

Soak the lentils together overnight, then strain and rinse with cold water. Place in a large saucepan with the water or stock and water and all the other ingredients. Simmer for 2 hours, or until tender. Remove the onion stuck with cloves and process the soup. Serve in bowls with a round of french bread fried in oil and garlic floating in each bowl. Freezes well.

LETTUCE OR LETTUCE & SORREL SOUP

This is a boon for those of you with a glut of 'bolting' lettuces, but if you live in a town you can always use up the outside leaves of lettuces which are too coarse to put in the salad.

4 oz (100g) peeled diced potato
2 oz (50g) peeled chopped onion
1 oz (25g) butter
1 lettuce roughly shredded (and 1 oz – 25g sorrel)
1 chicken stock cube and/or
1 pint (575ml) water or milk

or
1 pint stock (and omit stock cube and water)
1 dessertspoon sugar
salt and pepper to taste   Serves 4-6

'Sweat' the potato and onion in the butter until cooked but not coloured. Add the shredded lettuce (and sorrel if you are using some) stir and cook for a few seconds till limp. Then pour in the water or milk and stock cube or stock, cover and cook for 30 minutes or until tender. Liquidize or process until really smooth. If too thick add some milk. Adjust seasoning and serve. Also nice chilled and served with a swirl of cream in each soup cup. Freezes well.

MIXED VEGETABLE SOUP

It is difficult to give exact quantities or ingredients for this soup as it is what I call a 'turn out the fridge' soup. In other words you have odds and ends of vegetables in the bottom of the fridge of which there aren't enough to use on their own. This is just an example of the last one I made, but the next one might be slightly different.

1 onion	green trimmings from 2 leeks
1 outer stalk of celery	1 oz (25g) butter
1 carrot (wrinkly)	1 dessertspoon sugar
1 spoonful of cooked peas (left over from	water to cover
previous supper)	salt and pepper Serves 2-4

Peel the onion and potato, scrape the carrot and the stringy bits off the celery stalk and chop all the vegetables up finely, either by hand or in the Magimix. Put all the ingredients in a saucepan with the butter and about ¼ pint (150ml) water, cover and simmer until tender, about 20 minutes. Add water, cover and simmer for another 10 minutes. Serve as it is with a little grated cheese, or blend if a smoother soup is preferred. Freezes well.

MUSHROOM SOUP

This is designed for cultivated or field mushrooms, but if you are brave enough try making it with 'chanterelles'. These are bright orange and look like parasols that have blown inside out. Several years ago when on a fishing holiday in Scotland they were growing in profusion on the river bank, so, knowing the suspicious nature of my Archie and our fellow guests one of whom was Will Garfit, (the artist for this book), I made a delectable soup which they all enjoyed. When I told them afterwards they were quite horrified, but had to admit that it was delicious.

8 oz (225g) mushrooms (or chanterelles)	½ pint (275ml) milk
washed and drained	1 heaped teaspoon potato flour or cornflour
1 shallot or small onion finely chopped	1 dessertspoon sugar
2 oz (50g) butter	1 dessertspoon chopped parsley or tarragon
1 tablespoon lemon juice	salt and ground black pepper to taste
1 clove garlic	cream **4-6 servings**

Melt the butter over a low heat and add shallot and garlic. Chop the mushrooms or chanterelles in the food processor. Don't process them for too long, two twitches of the button is about enough. Add to the butter, shallot and garlic and cook for a few seconds, stirring well. Add lemon juice and cook for 5 minutes. Add the cornflour mixed in the milk and continue stirring until the soup thickens and comes to the boil. Add the sugar, seasoning and chopped parsley or tarragon. Swirl in some cream just before serving. Garlic croutons or crisply fried crumbled bacon added at the last minute make it a more substantial dish. Freezes well.

ONION SOUP

8 oz (225g) onions peeled and chopped
finely
2 oz (50g) butter
1 oz (25g) flour
1 pint (575ml) milk
½ chicken stock cube
1 heaped teaspoon sugar
salt and pepper to taste   **Serves 2-4**

Sauté the chopped onions in the butter over a very low heat until they are soft but not coloured. Sprinkle in the flour and cook for a minute or two, then take the pan off the stove and pour in the milk gradually, stirring constantly. Add the sugar, stock cube, salt and pepper and cook for 10 minutes over a very low heat, stirring occasionally so that it does not stick. Do not blend as the texture of this soup is what makes it so nice. You can serve it with fried croutons if you like, but I prefer the delicate flavour on its own. Freezes well.

OXTAIL SOUP

Another what I call 'main course' soup. It is very rich and filling and served with hot french bread and a salad makes a delicious lunch.

1 lb (450g) oxtail chopped in pieces and trimmed of fat
1 onion, peeled
1 leek
1 carrot
1 clove garlic
1 beef stock cube
1 oz (25g) butter

2 pints (1 litre) water
1 tablespoon tomato purée
1 tablespoon redcurrant jelly
1 oz (25g) beurre manié to thicken *p.19*
1 pinch mixed herbs
1 wine glass port or sherry
salt and ground black pepper   **Serves 6-8**

Brown the pieces of oxtail in the butter and remove to a casserole. Chop the onion, leek, carrot and garlic roughly and brown in the remaining butter. Add to the casserole together with the rest of the ingredients except the beurre manié and port or sherry. Place in a preheated oven at 300°F 150°C Gas Mark 2 for 3 to 4 hours or until the meat is falling off the bones. Strain and leave to get cold, then skim off the fat. Bring to the boil and add little pieces of beurre manié whisking continually until the soup is as thick as you require. Adjust the seasoning and add a wine glass of port or sweet sherry if you have it.

PUMPKIN SOUP

I can never think why this delicious soup is not more widely known. As far as I can see whenever you mention pumpkin to people, they either say 'Hallowe'en' or a dull, glazed look comes into their eyes and they mutter 'pumpkin pie' and 'don't Americans eat it at Thanksgiving?' If you live in a town, most greengrocers will be sure to have pumpkin or squash in the autumn, and in the country they are practically given away after 'Hallow'en'. Should you be landed with a 56lb pumpkin as I was last year you may have to commandeer a couple of extra preserving pans from your friends, but the following recipe just caters for those of you who buy it by the pound!

1 lb (450g) peeled and diced pumpkin
4 oz (100g) peeled chopped onion
4 oz (100g) peeled diced potato
1 clove garlic
1 chopped rasher bacon
2 oz (50g) butter
1 peeled and roughly chopped tomato
or
1 tablespoon tomato ketchup
1 heaped dessertspoon basil
1 dessertspoon sugar
1 beef stock cube
½ pint (275 ml) water
salt and ground black pepper   **Serves 4-6**

Melt the butter over a low heat and 'sweat' onion and potato until they are transparent. Add pumpkin, tomato, bacon, sugar, salt, stock cube and water. Cover and cook until soft. Add garlic which you have crushed in a garlic press and adjust seasoning. Squash with a potato masher and add the basil. Serve with croutons of fried bread. If you want a smoother and more delicate soup, omit the bacon and tomato and add a teaspoon of potato or cornflour mixed with a little milk to thicken the soup instead of the potato. Cook until it thickens and then process in the blender or Magimix until it is really smooth. Add some cream to each soup cup and garnish with a basil leaf, I personally prefer the more robust version. Freezes well.

SORREL SOUP

This is quite one of the most delicate and delicious soups I know. I grow it in my garden, but nicest of all is the wild sorrel which grows in old pasture and on downland. On holiday this year I found some growing all round the caravan we had rented in Scotland by Loch Awe, so was able to produce an epicurean meal of wild sorrel soup followed by freshly caught trout fried in butter and oatmeal.

4 oz (100g) sorrel (approximately a good handful)
4 oz (100g) peeled diced potato
2 oz (50g) peeled chopped onion
2 oz (50g) butter
½ pint (275ml) water
1 pint (575ml) milk
½ chicken stock cube
1 dessertspoon sugar

salt and pepper
¼ pint (150ml) single cream
2 egg yolks   Serves 6-8

'Melt' the potato and onion in the butter over a very low heat until soft and transparent. Shred the sorrel finely and add to the potato and onion, stir and cook for a few seconds then pour in the water and cover tightly. Simmer for 10 minutes or until completely tender. Add the sugar, stock cube, salt and pepper and process until really smooth. Thin down with milk until you have the right consistency. Reheat and just before serving add the egg yolks beaten up in the cream, but do not allow to boil or the soup will curdle. Freezes well.

SPINACH SOUP

1 lb (450g) fresh spinach or 1 packet frozen chopped spinach
1 shallot or small onion finely chopped
1 oz (25g) butter
½ chicken stock cube
1 pint (575ml) milk
To thicken, *either*
1 heaped teaspoon cornflour mixed with a little milk *or*
2 egg yolks beaten up in
⅛ pint (75ml) cream
1 teaspoon sugar
salt and pepper   Serves 6-8

Cook the shallot or onion in the butter until soft but not coloured. Add the washed and roughly chopped fresh spinach or the packet of frozen spinach and cook until tender (or thawed). Add the stock cube, milk, sugar and salt and pepper, then blend. Return to the pan, bring to the boil and pull off the stove. Add the cornflour or the egg and cream mixture and stir well. If using the latter do not allow the soup to boil when you reheat it or it will curdle. Freezes well.

WATERCRESS SOUP

1 bunch watercress
2 oz (50g) finely chopped onion
2 oz (50g) finely chopped potato
1 oz (25g) butter
½ chicken stock cube

1 pint (575ml) milk
¼ pint (150ml) water
1 teaspoon sugar
salt and white pepper to taste   Serves 4-6

Cook the onion and potato in the butter very gently until they become transparent. Pour in the water, crumble in the stock cube and simmer for 15 minutes. Drop the watercress into boiling salted water for 30 seconds, drain and chop roughly. Add to the potato and onion and tip into the blender or Magimix. Switch on and process until really smooth, then add the milk in a thin stream. Season and heat through. Serve hot or cold garnished with a swirl of cream and one or two watercress leaves in each soup cup. Freezes well.

GROUSE SOUP

1 old grouse (raw) or 4 grouse carcasses
(cooked)
1 carrot roughly chopped
1 onion roughly chopped
2 celery stalks sliced
1 rasher bacon snipped in pieces
1 oz (25g) butter
2 oz (50g) beurre manié p.19
1 teaspoon redcurrant jelly

1 teaspoon concentrated tomato purée
1 chicken stock cube
2 pints (1 litre) of water or stock (in which
case omit stock cube)
1 wine glass red wine
4 juniper berries
1 bayleaf
salt and pepper   **Serves 6-8**

Brown the grouse (or carcasses), bacon, carrot, onion and celery in the butter then remove to a casserole. Swirl the pan out with the red wine and scrape the bottom and sides to get off the brown bits. Add to the casserole together with the water and stock cube (or stock), juniper berries, bayleaf, jelly and tomato purée. Cover and cook in the oven at 300°F 150°C Gas Mark 2 for 2 hours. Strain and pour into a saucepan. Boil rapidly and reduce to 1½ pints (850ml). Now add small bits of beurre manié, whisking all the time until it thickens to the consistency you require. Serve piping hot. Optional – hand round sherry or madiera with the soup so that guests can help themselves. Freezes well.

WILD DUCK & ORANGE SOUP

2 duck carcasses (cooked)
1 carrot, roughly chopped
1 onion peeled and chopped
1 celery stalk sliced
1 teaspoon redcurrant jelly
1 stock cube
2 pints (1 litre) water or stock (in which case
omit stock cube)

1 wine glass sweet sherry or madeira
juice of ½ an orange
1 oz (25g) beurre manié (½ oz – 15g butter
and ½ oz – 15g flour kneaded together)
1 pinch mixed herbs
1 teaspoon grated orange rind   **Serves 4-6**

Put all the ingredients except the beurre manié and grated orange peel into a saucepan. Bring to the boil, then simmer until reduced to 1 pint (575ml). Strain and thicken with the beurre manié by dropping in little pieces at a time and whisking continuously. Colour with a spot of gravy browning if it looks anaemic. Adjust seasoning and serve with a pinch of grated orange peel in each soup cup. Freezes well.

PHEASANT CONSOMMÉ

This is particularly good if made with the carcass of Pheasant 'Guidwife', *p.61*. You can quite well serve it cloudy, but as I said earlier it is quite nice to show off sometimes, and your guests will be most impressed.

1 oz 2 pheasant carcasses (cooked)	2 pints (1 litre) water
1 carrot	1 wine glass red wine
1 onion, trimmed and cleaned but not	1 pinch mixed herbs
peeled (to give a good colour)	salt and pepper
1 celery stalk	2 egg whites and shells for clarifying
1 chicken stock cube	**Serves 4-6**

Put all the ingredients, except the egg whites and shells, into a saucepan, cover and simmer for 2 hours. Remove lid and boil rapidly until stock is reduced to 1½ pints (850ml). Strain into a clean saucepan and blot off all the fat with kitchen paper. Beat the egg whites up in a large pan with 1/3 of the stock until frothy, then pour in the rest of the hot, but not boiling, stock in a thin steady stream and add the egg shells. Place the pan over a moderate heat with the handle facing you. Agitate gently over the flame with a wire whisk *until it begins to simmer*. Now let it shiver for 15 minutes without stirring, give the handle a quarter turn to the left and continue until you complete the circle, letting it simmer for 15 minutes each time. After the last simmering let it rest for 15 minutes. Scald a clean tea towel and lay it in a colander or over a sieve. With a clean ladle scoop the soup carefully into the colander and let it drain. You should now have sparkling, clear, golden consommé. All the preceding instructions may sound rather complicated, but once you start clarifying the soup I think you will find it quite easy.

PIGEON & MUSHROOM CONSOMMÉ

5 pigeon carcasses made into stock as per	8 oz (225g) mushrooms, finely chopped
Pheasant Consommé in preceding recipe,	2 shallots finely chopped
but with the addition of	1 teaspoon redcurrant jelly
½ oz (15g) dried wild mushrooms (obtain-	1 wine glass port, madeira or sweet sherry
able from delicatessens and good Health	1 teaspoon oil
Food Stores.)	**Serves 4-6**

Simmer the mushrooms and shallot gently in the oil in a pan with a tightly fitting lid until they are soft. Pour in the pigeon stock, to which you have added a wine glass of port, madeira or sherry and a teaspoon redcurrant jelly and the dried wild mushrooms. Simmer for 1 hour. Strain and proceed to clarify as in the previous recipe for Pheasant Consommé. It is a very useful way of using up the carcasses once you have removed the breasts for either Escalopes *p.68*, or Pigeon Pâté *p.51*. It has a very subtle taste, and if your guests think of pigeon as a second class bird after tasting this, then let them think again!

Sauces

Roux based sauces

Sauces should never taste of flour. If they do you have not cooked the roux for long enough. 'What is a roux?' I hear you ask. It is the basis of all coating sauces and consists of equal quantities of flour and butter cooked together over a low heat for 2−3 minutes. The saucepan is then drawn off the stove and the liquid is poured in whilst the mixture is being stirred. This is the basic Béchamel Sauce, and from it spring any number of variations.

BÉCHAMEL SAUCE

1½ oz (40g) plain flour 1½ oz (40g) butter 1
pint (575ml) liquid, either milk or stock salt
and pepper

Melt the butter in a thick-bottomed pan over a moderate heat until it is frothing. Now sprinkle in the flour, blend and allow to cook for 2 minutes. Draw the pan off the stove and pour in about half the cold liquid very slowly, whisking all the time with a balloon whisk. When this has blended, pour in the rest of the liquid. Now draw the pan back onto the stove and continue to stir until the sauce thickens. Turn the heat right down and reduce by a third. Season to taste.

If the sauce looks lumpy, beat well with a whisk, and if this doesn't do the trick put the whole lot into the Magimix or blender.

CAPER SAUCE

This the classic sauce to go with Boiled Mutton. See *p. 74.*

2 oz (50g) butter	2 egg yolks
2 oz (50g) plain flour	salt and pepper to taste
1½ pints (850ml) liquor in which the leg of	
lamb was cooked	
1 tablespoon cream	

Proceed as for Béchamel Sauce, but just before pouring it over the leg of lamb heat up to just under boiling point, pull pan off the stove and whisk in the cream and egg yolk and add the capers.

MUSTARD SAUCE

Classic sauce for use with oily fish such as herring and mackerel.

1 oz (25g) plain flour	1 teaspoon vinegar
1 oz (25g) butter	1 dash Worcester sauce
¾ pint (425ml) milk	salt and pepper
1 good teaspoon made English mustard	

Follow the method for Béchamel Sauce and add the mustard, Worcester Sauce and vinegar at the end.

RICH ONION SAUCE

Use this as an accompaniment to Roast Leg of Lamb *p.74* instead of redcurrant jelly, or with Boiled Leg of Mutton *p.74* as a change from Caper Sauce *p.27*.

> 2 oz (50g) onion, peeled and finely chopped
> 1 oz (25g) butter
> 1 oz (25g) plain flour
> ½ pint (275ml) milk
> 1 tablespoon double cream
> salt and pepper

Melt the butter in a saucepan, add the chopped onion and cook over a very low heat until soft and transparent. Sprinkle in the flour and stir. Then continue as for Béchamel Sauce *p.27*. Just before serving add the cream.

PARSLEY SAUCE

Use with chicken or fish or as a basis for a fricassée of poultry or game.

> 1½ oz (40g) plain flour
> 1½ oz (40g) butter
> 1 pint (575ml) milk
> 1 tablespoon chopped parsley
> salt and pepper

Make a roux as for Béchamel Sauce, *p.27*. Pour in the milk slowly, whisking the whole time, off the stove. Pull the pan back onto a moderate heat and stir continuously until it thickens. Allow to cook for 5 minutes and then add the parsley and seasoning.

TARRAGON SAUCE

Especially good with chicken.

Make a Béchamel Sauce *p.27* with stock. After reducing, add ¼ pint (150ml) double cream in which you have mixed the yolks of 2 eggs and 1 tablespoon of chopped tarragon. Once you have added the cream and egg yolks do not allow the sauce to boil or it will curdle.

OTHER SAUCES

BREAD SAUCE

In this family, roast game and poultry *have* to be accompanied by bread sauce. If I did not produce a huge saucepan of bread sauce I believe there would be a 'demo' with everyone waving placards saying 'We Want Bread Sauce'. Many restaurants never seem to serve it nowadays and if they do it comes out of a packet and looks and tastes like a cross between a bread poultice and paperhanger's paste. The one we like is robust with plenty of onion — not one of your recipes where the onion, stuck with cloves (Oh! horrors!) is delicately steeped in the heated milk and then removed.

  6—8 slices of white bread, crusts cut off
  1 pint (575ml) milk
  1 onion roughly sliced
  1 oz (25g) butter, salt, and plenty of ground
  black pepper

Heat the milk together with the sliced onion until it comes to the boil. Process the breadcrumbs in blender or Magimix and tip them into the milk. Stir well, add seasonings and butter, cover and place over a very low heat for about 5 minutes. Pull to the side of the stove until needed. If too thin add more crumbs, if too thick add a drop of milk. This is a well seasoned, unctuous sauce. For a luxury version Lucy adds double cream.

HORSERADISH SAUCE

To make this sauce you must either grow your own horseradish (see *p. 15*) or beg some from a friend. It is quite different from the kind you get out of a bottle. If you have to grate it by hand, try and do it by an open window or your eyes will water and your nose will prickle, but if you have a blender or processor this makes the whole operation easier. To accompany Roast Beef *p. 71* or smoked trout.

> 1 oz (25g) cleaned and scraped horseradish
> root
> ½ pint (275ml) lightly whipped cream
> 1 teaspoon vinegar, salt to taste

Cut the horseradish into suitable pieces to go into the Magimix (or leave whole if grating by hand). Either use the blade or the *fine* grater. When grated/processed stir it into the whipped cream and add the other ingredients. Spoon into a screw top jar, fasten lid tightly and put in the fridge. Use immediately or it will lose its potency. Horseradish is at its strongest in the winter.

LUCY'S ASPARAGUS SAUCE

> 8 oz (225g) butter
> 3 yolks of hard−boiled egg
> 1½ whites of hard−boiled egg
>
> 3 small shallots
> 1 teaspoon lemon juice, salt, and pepper to
> taste

Melt the butter in a small pan, crumble in the egg yolks and stir until well amalgamated. Add the finely chopped shallots, chopped whites of egg, salt, pepper and lemon juice. Do not boil. Serve with asparagus, calabrese or broccoli spears. Also very good with fish. Father's comment − so it damn well should be, with all that butter!

TOMATO SAUCE

This is a basic sauce for all kinds of dishes but especially pasta. You can ring the changes with other herbs and omit the garlic if you are allergic to it.

> 1 lb (450g) tomatoes
> 8 oz (225g) onion, peeled and chopped
> 2 fat cloves garlic, chopped
> 1 tablespoon olive oil
>
> 1 dessertspoon chopped basil
> 1 teaspoon sugar
> 1 bayleaf, salt and ground black pepper

Plunge the tomatoes into boiling water, leave for 1 minute then transfer to a bowl of cold water. Fish them out, peel and take out the seeds. Heat the oil in a saucepan until it is smoking, throw in the onion and garlic, turn down the heat and cook for 5 minutes stirring continually. Now tip in the tomatoes, herbs and seasonings. Turn down the heat to very low and simmer gently for about 30 minutes, or until the mixture looks almost syrupy.

SHORT SAUCES

These are what the English call 'gravy', but bear little relation to the brown, glutinous stuff which used to be served in most households, hotels and restaurants. Things have got better, but there is still room for improvement.

These short sauces are based on the residue and juices from whatever you have been roasting, be it meat or fowl. As much fat as possible is poured off and the roasting pan is swirled out with a glassful of wine, white or red depending on whether you have cooked meat or poultry. All the brown bits are scraped off, then the liquid is poured into a small pan. You can then add a little vegetable water if it is not too salty, a little stock cube, and pepper. If you have cooked lamb, add a teaspoon of redcurrant jelly, if venison some rowan jelly, and cranberry jelly is delicious with roast grouse sauce. No hard and fast rules can be laid down, just experiment until you find the flavour you like. If you don't want to use wine, stock will be just as good. Should you wish to thicken your sauce slightly, (but not too much) just add a few scraps of beurre manié, *p. 19*.

WARM SAUCES

All 'warm' sauces are made basically with egg yolks and butter and different flavourings. They are always made in a 'Bain Marie' or bowl over hot, but not boiling water and should be served lukewarm and not hot or they will either curdle or turn into scrambled egg. If allowed to get cold they become quite hard as the butter solidifies.

In effect a 'warm sauce' is the same as mayonnaise only made with butter. The thickening process takes place as the butter is beaten into the warm egg yolks or, if made in the Magimix, the melted butter is dripped onto the whizzing egg yolks and flavouring. Once you get these principles into your head it should be quite easy, and the mystique of Béarnaise and Hollandaise will soon disappear when you have taken the plunge and tried them successfully. Capable cooks have been known to go quite pale at the thought of making either of these sauces. The great secret is to have all your ingredients ready and your time planned. The other tip is to have eggs which are several days old and are not absolutely new-laid. The same rule applies to mayonnaise and to meringues. Finally, do not take the eggs straight out of the fridge, but let them sit at room temperature for at least 2 hours.

CLASSIC BEARNAISE SAUCE 1

3−4 egg yolks
4−5 oz (100−150g) unsalt butter, or as required
2 shallots or 1 small onion
2 fl oz (60ml) white wine or water
2 tablespoons tarragon vinegar
1 tablespoon chopped tarragon
lemon juice
salt and pepper
ice cubes handy for disaster stakes! **Serves**
8−10 depending on greed of guests, and whether Archie is around!

Put wine, vinegar, shallots and pepper into a small saucepan. Reduce by fast boiling to 2 tablespoons. It is best to watch this like a hawk, as many is the time that I have turned my back, only to smell a burnt offering! You can do this reduction in the morning, pour it onto the egg yolks which have been broken into a small bowl, cover and leave until you need to make the sauce. Have your butter ready diced and some lemon juice into which you have put an ice cube. This is a precaution in case your sauce starts to curdle. Place the bowl with the egg yolks and reduced liquid over a saucepan of simmering water on a low heat. Add one or two bits of butter and keep whisking with a small balloon whisk until they melt. As the sauce thickens you can add more bits. When it is the consistency of thick double cream pull it off the stove. Add a few drops of lemon juice and if you want it to sit whilst you have a drink or your first course, drop a couple of bits of butter in, *don't* whisk and cover with foil. Just before serving, add the chopped tarragon and whisk in a few more bits of butter. If it starts to curdle, pull off the stove, take bowl out of saucepan and drop in an ice cube. When it has cooled the sauce slightly, fish it out. Whisk in another egg yolk and serve immediately.

BLENDER OR MAGIMIX BÉARNAISE 2

Use the same ingredients as for Béarnaise Sauce 1, *p. 31*. Tip the egg yolks and reduced vinegar into blender or Magimix. Melt half the butter until it is really hot but not foaming. Switch on the machine and pour in hot butter in a thin stream. When the yolks start to thicken, transfer to a bowl over hot water and proceed as for Béarnaise 1, adding bits of butter until it is as thick as you wish. You *can* complete the entire operation in the blender (in which case melt all the butter), but your sauce will be more of a single cream consistency.

HOLLANDAISE SAUCE

This is generally used with fish and egg dishes and as an alternative to melted butter with asparagus.

In relation to this sauce, I think the greatest devotion ever to the god Epicurus was shown by Lucy. When she was still at university two of her friends were doing a vacation job as ghillies on the river Grimester on the Island of Lewis. They were living in a bothy where the cooking conditions were primitive — only one small calor gas ring and no saucepans. The young men were allowed to catch one fish, which they duly did. With the salmon steaks fried in butter, Lucy served Hollandaise Sauce made in a large breakfast cup over hot water in the kettle. She said it was indeed a meal fit for the gods, as the salmon was so fresh it still had the milky curd which disappears after a very few hours.

3—4 egg yolks
1 tablespoon white wine
1 dessertspoon lemon juice
4—5 oz (100—150g) unsalted butter
salt and pepper

The method is slightly different to Béarnaise as you do not reduce the wine and lemon juice. Just pour them onto the egg yolks in the bowl. Place over hot water and keep adding the butter. Whisk well whilst you are doing this so that the sauce is light and frothy.

MAYONNAISE & SALAD DRESSINGS

CLASSIC MAYONNAISE 1

This is a virtually foolproof method of making mayonnaise providing you don't use very new-laid eggs straight out of the fridge. The oil and egg yolks should both be at room temperature. If you do have a failure, don't despair. Simply pour the 'failed' mayonnaise into a jug, break 2 more egg yolks into the bowl, add mustard and pour in the 'failure' very gradually. You will generally find that this works, but sometimes if the weather is very sultry and thundery you may have to concede defeat and have a very rich kind of salad dressing!

2 egg yolks
1 level teaspoon mild Dijon mustard
½ pint (275ml) sunflower or olive oil
1 dessertspoon wine vinegar or lemon juice
½ teaspoon sugar
¼ teaspoon salt & pepper

Separate the egg yolks from the whites and place in a bowl with the seasonings. Beat well with a wire whisk or fork. Start pouring in the oil drop by drop until the mixture begins to thicken. Once this happens you can start pouring faster. When the mayonnaise has reached an almost jelly-like consistency then add the vinegar or lemon juice. You can use electric hand beaters but you won't get that voluptuously velvety look which you get at any little restaurant in France.

BLENDER OR MAGIMIX MAYONNAISE 2

This is very economical as you use the whole of an egg and not just the yolk, but it has more the texture and taste of salad cream and is particularly good for use with potato salad.

1 whole egg
1 level teaspoon made mustard
½ pint (275ml) sunflower or olive oil
1 dessertspoon wine vinegar
½ teaspoon sugar
¼ teaspoon salt pepper

Break the egg into the liquidizer or Magimix, add seasonings. Switch on to high and start pouring in the oil in a thin, steady stream. When the mayonnaise begins to thicken, pour a bit faster until you have used up all the oil and then add the vinegar. A tablespoon of boiling water will help if you want to keep it in a screw top jar in the fridge.

MAYONNAISE VARIATIONS SAUCE FRANÇOISE

Classic Mayonnaise 1 *p.33* to which you stir in:

1 dessertspoon brandy
2 tablespoons tomato sauce
1 tablespoon Worcester Sauce
2–3 drops Tabasco sauce

This makes a different sauce with which to dress prawn cocktails.

SAUCE MALTAISE

Make Classic Mayonnaise 1, *p.33* but omit vinegar. Use instead:

1 teaspoon lemon juice
1 tablespoon orange juice (preferably Seville)

grated peel of 1 orange
1 egg white stiffly beaten
1 tablespoon double cream

Seville orange is best, but you can only get them during the season, otherwise use a sweet orange. You can also use a tangerine, which gives a very delicate flavour and goes particularly well with cold fillet of pork sliced very thinly on a dish. Dribble the sauce down the centre and serve the rest separately.

TARTARE SAUCE

To be served with deep fried fish.

Mayonnaise 1 or 2 *p.33* to which you add:
1 finely chopped shallot or 1 small onion
1 or 2 finely chopped gherkins
1 teaspoon chopped capers

1 dessertspoon finely chopped parsley,
or as a variation use dill, fennel or tarragon

COOKED CHICKEN SALAD DRESSING

This is a delicious dressing for Chicken Salad *p.85* and with the addition of aspic or gelatine it can be used as a Chaudfroid for coating cold poultry or game.

½ cup of concentrated chicken stock
½ cup wine vinegar
5 egg yolks, slightly beaten
2 tablespoons made English mustard
1 teaspoon salt

¼ teaspoon pepper
pinch cayenne
½ cup thick cream
⅓ cup melted butter

Put all the ingredients except the cream and butter into the top of a double boiler or in a bowl over a saucepan of hot water. Cook until the mixture begins to thicken, stirring constantly Add cream and butter and cool.
Variations
Chaudfroid
You can use tarragon vinegar instead of plain vinegar, add 1 tablespoon chopped tarragon and ¼ pint (150 ml) aspic. When the sauce has cooled but not set you can use it as a Chaudfroid, or coating sauce for chicken or turkey breasts. If the stock you are using is jellied then you can omit the aspic.
Cold Béarnaise Sauce Use 1 cup tarragon vinegar, throw in 2 shallots or 1 medium onion and reduce by fast boiling to ½ cup.
Curried Sauce Use plain vinegar, add curry powder to taste and 1 dessertspoon mango chutney juice. This makes a sort of Coronation Chicken with a difference.

COATS SALAD DRESSING

Another of Archie's 'specials' − anyone watching either of us making this dressing is usually amazed at the amount of sugar which goes in, but the end result is quite delicious. A French friend whose family are very orthodox in their tastes tentatively tried it out on them and it is now their standard dressing.

1 heaped teaspoon Dijon mustard
or Archie's Mustard *p.18*.
1 tablespoon sugar
1 dessertspoon wine vinegar

5 tablespoons oil
pinch minced garlic or garlic powder
(optional)
salt and pepper

With a small whisk or a fork mix together the mustard, sugar, vinegar and seasonings. Add oil and beat well until the dressing becomes really thick. Keeps well in the fridge. If you use Archie's Mustard, omit the pinch of garlic.

GRAVADLAX MUSTARD & DILL SAUCE

This sauce is primarily to go with Gravadlax *p. 44 but it is equally good with plain grilled herring or mackerel.*

1 tablespoon mild Dijon Mustard
1 tablespoon demerara sugar
1 tablespoon vinegar
½ pint (275ml) olive oil

1 tablespoon fresh chopped dill, frozen dill
or dried dill
salt and pepper

Put the mustard into a bowl with the sugar, salt and pepper and gradually beat in the oil with a fork or small whisk. Finally stir in the dill. Keeps in the fridge in a screw top jar for up to a week.

SAUCE GRIBICHE

This is delicious with avocado pear as a starter *p. 37*, with cold calabrese, and with cold smoked trout.

3 hardboiled eggs
1 level teaspoon Dijon mustard
1 tablespoon chopped parsley, chives and
chervil

¼ pint (150ml) olive oil vinegar or lemon
juice
salt and freshly ground black pepper

Separate the yolks and white. Mash the yolks together with the herbs and seasonings and add the oil a drop at a time, increase to steady stream and when it finally begins to thicken add vinegar or lemon juice to taste, and finally the chopped egg whites. This sauce will not be thick like mayonnaise. Don't worry if the oil separates — it doesn't matter.

REMOULADE 1

Use with prawns or fried or grilled fish as a change from Sauce Tartare *p. 34.*

1 hard boiled egg yolk
1 egg yolk
1 dessertspoon mild Dijon mustard

2 tablespoons tarragon vinegar
¼ pint (150ml) olive oil
salt and pepper

Mix the two egg yolks with the mustard and seasonings. Add the oil slowly and finally the vinegar.

REMOULADE SAUCE 2 (FOR CELERIAC)

If you have ever sat on the sidewalk in a small restaurant in France in summer and chosen hors d'oeuvres, the chances are that you will have been offered crunchy julienne strips of celeriac in a delicately creamy, mustardy sauce. In your innocence you will have assumed as I did that this is a kind of mayonnaise. Not so, as there are no egg yolks, but the method is the same. It took me a long time to discover the secret — it is made with mild Dijon mustard, but nevertheless does not taste in the least bit hot. *See p. 85.*

4 tablespoons mild Dijon mustard
3 tablespoons boiling water
¼–½ pint (150–275ml) olive oil
2 tablespoons white wine vinegar
salt and pepper
1 tablespoon double cream (optional)

Warm bowl, liquidizer goblet or Magimix bowl. Put in mustard, add water drop by drop and then the oil, as for mayonnaise. Finally add vinegar, salt and pepper and the cream.

SALSA VERDE

This pungent and strongly flavoured sauce goes extremely well with cold roast veal, which can be a bit insipid otherwise. It is also excellent with cold salmon.

    1 small chopped onion
    1 clove chopped garlic
    4 capers chopped
    1 hard boiled egg, chopped
    1 anchovy chopped
    1 cup chopped parsley
    1 tablespoon blanched and drained water-
    cress or spinach wrung out in a towel and
    then finely chopped
    1 tablespoon vinegar
    4 tablespoons olive oil
    salt and freshly ground black pepper

Combine all the ingredients except the oil and vinegar. Add these last.

VINAIGRETTE SAUCE

Classic salad dressing for those who do not like it quite so sweet as the Coats' recipe. Use the avocado and anything rather rich which needs a tart sauce.

    4 tablespoons olive oil,
    sunflower or flavoured herb oil *p. 17.*
    1 dessertspoon vinegar or lemon juice
    ½ teaspoon mustard
    ½ teaspoon sugar
    salt and pepper

Mix all ingredients together and stir whilst pouring so as to incorporate everything. Probably best poured into a bottle with a screw top so that you can shake it up each time you use it. Keeps in the fridge for up to a week.

Starters & Egg Dishes

A meal should be well balanced if possible. I remember that soon after we came to live here I had a dinner party and invited a rather intimidating lady and her husband. When we had left the men to their port she informed me that although my dinner had been excellent in many ways, I had committed the cardinal sin of using the same ingredient in two of the courses – I had put cream in the first course and the pudding. In the same way it is best if possible to avoid serving courses that are all the same colour. This happened to my mother and father before the war when they dined with the late Lord Rosebery at Mentmore Towers. The entire dinner was served on gold plates and all six courses were pink!

AVOCADOES WITH SAUCE GRIBICHE

Time was when avocadoes were a rarity and scarcely seen outside a grand restaurant. Now they are quite commonplace and can be found almost anywhere. The following recipe makes a nice change and is economical as 2 fair sized avocadoes make enough for 6–8 people.

2–3 avocadoes
Sauce Gribiche p. 35   **Serves 6–8**

Cut the avocadoes in half, take out the stones, peel and cut in small dice. Mix in with the sauce. Add more vinegar or lemon juice if you think it necessary. Divide into ramekins.

CALABRESE VINAIGRETTE

Archie and I both prefer to eat this as a starter rather than as a vegetable so that we get the full benefit of the delicate and special flavour. It is equally good hot with melted butter. If you have a garden and grow Curly Kale, the little shoots which appear after you have removed the centre are quite delicious done this way as are the young spears of purple sprouting broccoli or asparagus.

1 bunch Calabrese weighing about 1 lb
(450g)
6 tablespoons Vinaigrette Sauce p. 36
or if served hot
6 tablespoons melted butter,
Hollandaise Sauce p. 32
or Lucy's Asparagus Sauce p. 30   **Serves 4**

Trim the calabrese into 3″ (7½cm) lengths and cook in boiling salted water for 5 minutes – they should be firm but tender. Divide amongst 4 ramekins and when cold pour over vinaigrette sauce.

BAKED EGGS

For some reason, lost in the mists of time this has become the Coats' traditional Sunday breakfast, but, of course it is really a starter.

6 eggs
1 oz (25g) butter
6 thin streaky rashers of smoked bacon, crisply fried

6 dessertspoons double cream
6 good pinches of Lawry's or Schwartz
Seasoned Salt and Archie's Pepper p. 18 or ground black pepper

Preheat oven to 400°F/200°C Gas Mark 6. Divide the butter amongst 6 ramekins and place in the oven to melt. When the butter is foaming break in the eggs, cover with the cream and season. Put in the top of the oven for 5 minutes. Take out and serve immediately either as they are or with the crisply fried bacon crumbled over the top.

CELESTINE'S STARTER

This is rather rich and filling so use small 3″ (7½cm) ramekins. Celestine's original recipe gave 2 lb smoked salmon which seemed to me both expensive and excessive so I cut it down to half.

1 lb (450g) smoked salmon
2 ripe avocadoes (small Hassler – the dark brown ones with rough skin)
¼ pkt Philadelphia cream cheese
dash of Tabasco Sauce

5 drops Worcester Sauce
juice ¼ lemon
salt and pepper
Garnish
black Lumpfish roe (Danish Caviar)

Serves 6—8

Oil 6 ramekins, then line them with the smoked salmon, making sure that there is enough to overlap the rims. Purée together the avocadoes, philadelphia cheese, lemon juice and seasonings. Fill each ramekin with the mousse and fold the smoked salmon over the top. Cover with cling film and refrigerate for 4 hours or overnight. Turn out and garnish with a slice of lemon and a teaspoonful of black Lumpfish roe.

CHERVILLED EGGS

6 hard boiled eggs
½ pint (275ml) mayonnaise (recipe 1 or 2 see p.33)
1 tablespoon chopped fresh, or crumbled

frozen chervil
additional salt and pepper if necessary
paprika for garnishing   **Serves 6**

Cut the eggs up roughly in fairly large pieces into a bowl. Mix in the mayonnaise and chervil and add some more salt and pepper if you think it necessary. This dish should be on the sloppy side, so you may have to add some more mayonnaise. Divide into 6 ramekins and sprinkle a tiny bit of paprika on top of each. If you are feeling lazy or are pushed for time, use Hellman's instead of home-made mayonnaise.

OEUFS POCHÉS HENRI IV

We first tasted this delicate dish with the same friend who started us on the strawberry business. It was the first time that Lucy then aged five, had ever been to London, let alone the River Room restaurant at the Savoy Hotel. A satin cushion to sit on, and the Head Waiter dancing attendance set the seal on her future expensive tastes, and she has never looked back!

6–8 poached eggs, or soft-boiled eggs done for 5–6 minutes
6–8 shortcrust pastry rounds

Sauce Béarnaise as per recipe p.31
Serves 6—8

Poach or boil the eggs in the morning and leave in a bowl of water.

Shortcrust Pastry

6 oz (175g) plain flour
3 oz (75g) cold, unsalt butter
1 oz (25g) lard
2 tablespoons water

Sift flour into bowl or Magimix, add butter and lard cut in small pieces and process or rub in until it resembles fine crumbs. (15 seconds in the Magimix). Add water until the pastry forms a ball. Roll out and cut into the requisite number of rounds. Prick with a fork and bake at 400°F 200°C Gas Mark 6 for 5−8 minutes. (Make a few extra in case of breakages.)

While you have been making the sauce the poached/soft-boiled eggs should have been transferred to a bowl of hot, but not boiling water and the pastry rounds should have been gently warmed through in the oven.

If your guests are due to arrive at 8 o'clock p.m. for 8.15, start making the sauce at 7.45 which should, if all goes well, leave you time to greet them and knock back a large drink before returning to the kitchen.

When the sauce is ready, herd your guests into the dining room, place a pastry round in each warmed ramekin, place an egg on each (having drained and dried gently with a clean tea towel). Cover liberally with sauce and serve immediately. If Archie is around be sure to have some extra sauce as it's almost his favourite dish and he always asks for more and would eat it by the tablespoon if he was allowed.

If you wish to impress your guests even more, use 2 soft-boiled quail's eggs per person instead of a hen's egg. These are the devil to get just right, but I find if you place them in a saucepan of cold water, bring it to the boil, then turn off and let them sit in the water for 1 minute before taking them out and plunging them into cold water. It generally works.

RUMBLED EGGS WITH CHOPPED SAUTÉED CHICKEN LIVERS

You may recall that Archie was in Paris before the war, supposedly learning French and cooking. He kept on talking about the Oeufs Brouillés aux Foies de Volaille which he had eaten at La Crémaillère. Every time I tried to make it he said it wasn't quite right. Finally, one day Lucy made her special scrambled eggs – learnt when cooking for her godfather in Spain. 'Hooray' cried Archie on eating the first mouthful, 'you've cracked it'! 'Cracked what?' we said. 'The Crémaillère scrambled eggs with chicken livers,' was the reply. (Technically they are called rumbled eggs because they are made in a bain marie over hot water.)

6 eggs beaten
3 oz (75g) butter
salt and freshly ground black pepper
3 oz (75g) chicken livers   **Serves 4−6**

Remove the stringy bits from the livers, cut them up quite small and sauté in 1 oz (25g) of the butter. Set aside. Melt the rest of the butter in a bowl over a pan of hot water and then add the eggs. Stir constantly with a wire whisk over a low heat until the eggs become creamy and set.

Have ready 4 rounds of toast, pour a little of the butter from the sauté pan onto each, fold the livers into the egg mixture and divide. This will be enough for 4−6 people for a starter or for 2 people as a supper dish. You can if you like omit the toast and serve in small ramekins.

'SHOOTABLE STAG' or DEVILLED KIDNEYS

This has nothing to do with stags or deer stalking. It is merely an euphemism to describe the extremely attractive girl who gave the following recipe to Archie. It is a very versatile recipe as you can serve it as a starter or a savoury, or increase the quantities and you have a delicious main course to be accompanied by rice or mashed potatoes. You do, however, have to know beforehand whether your guests will a) eat offal, or b) eat curry.

4 lamb's kidneys
1 dessertspoon Worcester Sauce
2 oz (50g) butter
1 teaspoon each of: curry powder
made English mustard
plain flour
tomato ketchup
lemon juice
salt, cayenne pepper   **Serves 4**

Trim kidneys and cut each into 4. Roll in flour. Heat butter over a low flame and add lemon juice, Worcester Sauce, tomato ketchup and seasonings. Tip in the kidneys and cook over a very low heat until they are just done and still pink in the middle. Serve on squares of hot, buttered toast. Can be prepared in the morning and heated up in the evening. Freezes well, but if you are going to do this be sure to undercook them as by the time you have reheated them they will be just right.

MOUSSES

Mousses are a great standby and most of them freeze well except for the ones containing chopped hard-boiled egg. I have two basic recipes and play around with different flavours and combinations. The following was the first one I ever attempted and the original recipe contained condensed milk, but that was because rationing was still partially on and you could only get cream as a rare treat – so much so that on about the fourth day of our honeymoon in Ireland which was flowing with butter, cream, and steak, Archie ate so much that he had a bilious attack. Anyway I now use cream, but the condensed milk gave a jolly good flavour and I sometimes think it tasted even better.

CRAB MOUSSE

8 oz (225g) crab meat, fresh, frozen or
tinned.
3 eggs
¼ pint (150ml) milk
bayleaf, onion ring, pinch mixed herbs, 6
peppercorns, salt
small piece of garlic (optional)
½ oz (15g) gelatine
2 tablespoons mayonnaise
½ pint (275ml) cream, whipped
salt, pepper, pinch cayenne   **Serves 6–8**

Put egg yolks, milk, bayleaf, slice of onion, herbs, peppercorns and garlic in a small bowl over a pan of hot water. Stir constantly over a low heat until the mixture begins to thicken. Mix in the crab meat and add the gelatine which you have dissolved in a very little hot, but not boiling, water. Spoon into a larger bowl and allow to cool. When cold enough fold in the whipped cream and when the mixture just begins to set fold in the 3 egg whites stiffly beaten. Pour into a straight sided soufflé dish or individual ramekins and put in the fridge. The original recipe said to serve Sauce Tartare with it, but I think it was rather gilding the lily, so I just serve it on its own.

Short cut. If you are in a hurry, place the bowl of crab mixture, whipped cream and gelatine in a larger bowl containing some ice cubes. Stir occasionally until the mixture begins to thicken. At this point fold in the stiffly beaten whites of egg. If you are not in a hurry, don't bother about the ice cubes, but just put the bowl in the fridge to cool. Don't forget it though, or you will find it has set rock hard and you cannot fold in the egg whites.

CHEESE MOUSSE

Rather a filling mousse, so best served in small individual ramekins.

Follow the recipe for Crab Mousse *p.40* but instead of crab add 8 oz (225g) grated cheddar cheese to the 'custard' mixture. Stir until it has melted, but take care that it doesn't turn into scrambled egg. It is best to pull the pan off the stove while you are doing this.

SMOKED HADDOCK MOUSSE

As per the basic recipe, but substitute 8 oz (225g) cooked smoked haddock for the crab meat. Use the milk in which you have cooked the fish to make your 'custard' but omit salt. Chopped hard-boiled egg makes a nice addition to this mousse and/or 2oz (50g) grated cheese.

SPINACH MOUSSE

To the basic recipe add:

1×8 oz (225g) packet frozen chopped spinach, unthawed	¼ pint (150ml) Béchamel Sauce *p.27*
2 shallots finely chopped	1 pinch oregano
1 oz (25g) butter	1 pinch nutmeg
	salt and pepper

Melt the butter in a saucepan over a low heat and cook the shallots in it until tender – about 5 minutes. Add the spinach and continue cooking until all the liquid has evaporated, then add the Béchamel Sauce and the 'custard'. Cool, and proceed as before.

Optional additions 1 tablespoon finely chopped ham, 1 tablespoon grated cheese, chopped hard-boiled egg.

EGG MOUSSE

This is a very light mousse and the method of making it is totally different as, except for the hard—boiled eggs it requires no cooking so is a great boon if you are pushed for time.

6 hard—boiled eggs	1 teaspoon Harvey's Sauce
½ pint (275ml) cream, whipped	1 teaspoon Anchovy essence
1 tin Campbell's condensed consommé, or 5 heaped teaspoons aspic dissolved in a little sherry	1 pinch cayenne
	1 pinch Lawry's or Schwartz Seasoned Salt
	1 pinch curry powder
1 teaspoon Worcester Sauce	salt and ground black pepper **Serves 6–8**

Place the yolks of hard-boiled egg in the Magimix or blender together with the seasonings, consommé or aspic and blend. Pour into a bowl, add the roughly chopped egg whites and then fold in the whipped cream. Spoon into individual ramekins, place in the fridge and allow to set.

Variations
KIPPER MOUSE As above but omit curry powder. Add instead Lemon Pepper or lemon juice and the flesh of 2 cooked kippers minus bones and skin.

SARDINE MOUSSE
Add to the Egg Mousse 2 tins of sardines drained of oil, ½ teaspoon curry powder and 1 tablespoon chutney.

SMOKED TROUT MOUSSE

If you have a smoker you can either catch or buy your trout and smoke them yourself. But failing this you can buy smoked trout quite easily from the larger supermarkets and from good fishmongers. It makes a delicious mousse.

8 oz (225g) smoked trout, skinned and
boned
½ pint (275ml) cream whipped
1 teaspoon lemon juice
3 heaped teaspoons aspic dissolved in ½ pint
(275ml) boiling water
1 teaspoon dill weed
salt and freshly ground black pepper
Optional: Lumpfish roe to garnish

Blend the trout, lemon juice, half the aspic, dill and seasoning until smooth. Pour into a bowl and fold in the whipped cream and spoon into a soufflé dish or individual ramekins. Put in the fridge. When set pour a thin layer of the remaining aspic over the top. When jellied decorate with a thin slice of lemon and a few grains of Lumpfish roe and pour a final layer of aspic over the top. Serve with thin slices of granary or rye bread and butter.

Fish

Archie is now unfortunately only able to fish from a boat, but we are lucky enough to be able to race up the motorway to Ashmere, where Jean and Keith Howman, together with Colin Willock produce the necessary craft. Getting Archie into the boat is quite a feat, as he is on crutches. So far we have managed it without either of us falling in. As the Master lowers himself gingerly onto his rubber pigeon shooting cushion in the stern the boat goes down at an alarming angle, due to his girth, which is rather large. I am by no means a featherweight, but even so the sharp end seems to point skywards in rather a frightening manner. The last time we went out it was just as well Archie couldn't see behind him, because there was only about 2″ freeboard. I was manoevring the boat when he got into his first fish and he got a very wet backside as we shipped a lot of water!

The 'farmed' trout that you see on your fishmonger's slab is really best smoked. That is to say 'hot smoked', as I have described under the heading of Smoked Pigeon Pâté *p. 53*.

When I smoke this kind of trout I usually salt them and sprinkle some dill weed or fennel on top. If you catch or are given a large rainbow trout it is nice to have it properly 'cold-smoked', in which case it tastes much like smoked salmon. Don't try and do this yourself or you may have the kind of disaster I once had. I rigged up a sort of wigwam in the garden, covered it with wire netting and then with sacks, lit the sawdust underneath and hung my salmon from the top. The first two smokings were fine, but the third and final one came to a sticky end. Archie called me to do something to the Land Rover. By the time I got back a wind had sprung up and set the whole wigwam on fire and my tenderly and carefully cured fish was just a 'burnt offering'! Anyone thinking of 'having a go' at cold smoking would be well advised not to follow my example but to ask my old friend Colin Willock, who is the real expert. He has written extensively in the *Shooting Times* on the trials and tribulations of being a DIY home smoker.

The true wild 'brownie' caught in a highland burn or loch only needs to be filleted, coated in oatmeal and fried in butter, with perhaps a rasher or two of bacon. This is all that is necessary to bring out the delicious nutty flavour.

Try and find a fishmonger who sells fresh, not frozen fish. It should smell of the sea – I can only describe it as a sort of 'seaweedy' smell. Avoid anything that smells of ammonia like the plague as this means it is stale.

CREVETTES THÉODORE

We came across this on our first wedding anniversary, at a little Greek restaurant in Kensington, which sadly doesn't exist any more. It is quite delicious and, provided you have the main ingredients in your freezer, can be made in 10 minutes flat. It should be made with Young's potted shrimps but as these are difficult to find and very expensive you may have to make your own.

POTTED PRAWNS

8 oz (225g) frozen peeled prawns (or shrimps if you can get them).
4 oz (100g) unsalt butter, clarified

½ teaspoon ground mace
1 teaspoon ground nutmeg
ground black pepper and salt if necessary

Thaw the prawns completely, drain well and put in the food processor. Chop for two short bursts. Don't do this if you are using shrimps. Whilst they are thawing clarify the butter by placing it in a small pan with 1 tablespoon of water over a very low heat. Bring to the boil, skim off the white foam flecks. Pour into a pyrex jug or bowl. Cool and put in the freezer for half an hour. Take out and remove the, by now, hard butter and throw away the liquid which has formed underneath. Heat the clarified butter in a pan and add the chopped prawns (or whole shrimps) and all the seasonings. Heat slightly but do not boil, then pull pan off the stove and leave to steep for half-an-hour. Pour into a pot, cool and refrigerate.

CREVETTES THÉODORE

4 x 2 oz (50g) pots Young's potted shrimps (or the home-made version)
1 oz (25g) butter
2 fl oz (60ml) sherry

3 tablespoons concentrated tomato purée
2–3 tablespoons freshly grated parmesan
½ teaspoon Italian mixed herbs

Melt the butter in a pan until just foaming, add all the ingredients except the cheese and heat quickly, stirring constantly. Add the cheese last and serve *immediately* on squares of toast or in individual ramekins. You can increase the quantity and serve as a main course with rice. If it becomes a bit oily, you can counteract this by adding a teaspoon of potato flour or cornflour mixed with a little water.

GRAVADLAX

This is the age old Scandinavian method of preserving salmon and is an ideal recipe for anyone without a home smoker. You can use salmon, trout or mackerel and it makes a nice change from smoked fish. The recipe I give is for trout as if we are lucky enough to catch or be given salmon we prefer to eat it plain or have it cold smoked.

1 x 2 lb (900g) rainbow or brown trout
2 tablespoons demerara sugar
2 tablespoons coarse sea salt
2 tablespoons dill, fresh, frozen or dried
1 teaspoon crushed white peppercorns
Optional: a few drops of brandy, aquavit or
vinegar

Step 1 Cut off the head of the trout, lay it on its side with the tail towards you and the backbone to your right (reverse procedure if left–handed). With a sharp knife slit down the backbone and with the point of the knife keep easing the flesh away, pulling gently to the left with your left hand, easing and scraping until you have exposed one side of the rib cage.
Step 2 Insert the point of the knife beneath the tail end of the backbone which you then lift with your left hand. Keep easing the knife underneath the backbone until you get to the rib cage. Ease the knife underneath this until you can pull the whole backbone and rib cage out in one, together with the innards.
Step 3 Lay the fish out flat, skin side down and go over it carefully for any bones you may have missed – a pair of pointed pliers or even eyebrow tweezers are a help. It is very important to remove all the bones completely or you will find it impossible to slice properly.
Step 4 Now mix the dill and all the dry ingredients together and spread them evenly over the fish. Sprinkle with a few drops of brandy, aquavit or vinegar if you like.

Step 5 Fold the fish over, skin outside, lay on a dish, place a board on top and then an 8 lb (4kg) weight. This is vital. The first time I made this dish I did not use a heavy enough weight. The texture of the finished article was flaky, and I could not slice it tidily.

Step 6 Leave in a cool place or in the bottom of your fridge for 24 hours. Open out, drain off the liquid and scrape off the dill and peppercorns. Slice diagonally in ¼″ (1cm) slices. Lay them on a dish and try and arrange them so that the fish looks reconstituted. Sprinkle generously with more dill, garnish with lemon slices and serve with Gravadlax Mustard and Dill Sauce *p. 35* and buttered dark rye bread or pumpernickel.

HERRINGS IN OATMEAL

Nothing could be more delicious or filling than fresh herrings grilled with oatmeal. Some people object to the bones (including my family who can be guaranteed to find a bone in a fish finger). But most of these can be avoided if you get your fishmonger to fillet them and split them open, or, follow the instructions for boning trout in the recipe for Gravadlax *p. 44*. When choosing them try and buy medium sized fish, not the great big monsters which tend to be coarse, nor the small ones which can be tasteless. The best time to eat them is May and June when they are in the best condition. Do try and get them fresh if you can.

4 herrings, beheaded and filleted
medium oatmeal for sprinkling
1 oz (25g) butter   **Serves 2–4**

Sprinkle the herrings with the oatmeal. Melt the butter in the grill pan and lay the fish in the pan skin side up, you may have to sprinkle on a little more oatmeal. Cook under a hot preheated grill until the skin begins to turn brown. Flip over and leave under the grill until the oatmeal colours. Serve with Mustard Sauce *p. 27* and new or mashed potatoes. Nothing else is needed as they are very rich.

MACKEREL

These can be cooked in the same way as herrings, but as they are, if anything, even richer, I prefer to cook them whole and serve with butter and lemon juice.

4 medium sized mackerel – these must be *absolutely fresh*
oil

salt and pepper
2 oz (50g) butter melted with 1 teaspoon
lemon juice   **Serves 2–4**

Take the heads off the mackerel and take out the innards, or get your fishmonger to do it for you. Cut three or four diagonal slits on each side of the fish. Rub with a little oil, salt and pepper. Preheat the grill and cook under a medium heat until the skin is brown and rising in little bubbles. Turn fish over and repeat on the other side. Serve with the melted butter and lemon juice separately and sprinkle with chopped parsley.

MOCK WHITEBAIT or GOUJONS OF FISH

Ever since we have been married, which is thirty-five years, Archie has been badgering me to cook him something called 'Mock Whitebait', which he used to have at his old home in Scotland. I really had no idea what he meant. The light suddenly dawned when we were out to dinner and our hostess gave us 'Goujons of Sole'. The cry went up, 'This is it.' 'What?' I asked, somewhat mystified. 'Mock Whitebait,' he said. So the problem was solved. It is very easy to do, can be prepared and put in the freezer, is very filling and so therefore economical.

2 fillets of lemon sole or plaice
plain flour for dredging
dried breadcrumbs (preferably undyed) for coating
1 egg beaten well with 1 tablespoon of milk

oil for frying
Serves 2 as a main course Serves 4 as a starter

Cut each fillet lengthwise down the middle and then diagonally across in ½″ (2cm) strips. Dredge with flour (ie roll in or pat with flour till covered and shake off excess), dip in beaten egg and milk and then coat in breadcrumbs. Heat the oil in a frying pan or chip pan until it is smoking hot and then throw in several 'goujons'. Cook until crisp and golden, about 2 minutes. Lift out with a slotted spoon and place on kitchen paper. Continue until you have cooked them all. Eat immediately or they will go soggy. If using as a main course serve with plenty of brown bread and butter and a plain green salad and Tartare Sauce *p.34*.
As a starter serve with lemon wedges and Sauce Françoise *p.33*.

SALMON MAYONNAISE

It may sound extravagant, but nowadays you can buy 'farmed' salmon quite reasonably. If you buy the tail end it may be even cheaper. You should get a piece weighing about 2 lb (900g). Place in a pan and cover with cold water. Add 1 teaspoon of salt. Bring to simmering point very slowly and cook for 5 minutes, then allow to get quite cold in the liquid. Take out, skin and take the flesh off the backbone, you will get 4 fillets – 2 off each side. Take 2 and arrange each on a plate. Garnish with thinly sliced cucumber. Serve with Mayonnaise 1 *p.33* or Salsa Verde *p.36* and Russian Salad *p.87*. Make the remaining 2 fillets into salmon fishcakes, using the recipe for Smoked Trout Fishcakes *p.47* or Salmon Kedgeree *p.46*.

In total you should be able to feed 6–8 people from this piece of salmon so it is quite economical.

SALMON KEDGEREE

An alternative way of using up cold salmon. Luxurious for breakfast or 'brunch' and delicious for supper.

    2 fillets of cooked tail end of salmon approx
    12 oz (350g)
    2 hard-boiled eggs, roughly chopped
    6 oz (175g) Basmati or long grained rice, or
    3 sachets of Uncle Ben's precooked rice
    3 oz (75g) butter
    ¼ pint (150ml) cream
    salt and ground black pepper
    chopped parsley to garnish   **Serves 2–4**

If using Basmati or long grained rice, heat a dessertspoon oil in a saucepan. When hot tip in the rice and stir until it is all coated. Pour in boiling water to 1″ (3cm) above the rice. Add ½ teaspoon salt and cover tightly with a lid. Turn heat right down and cook until all the water has been absorbed. Remove from stove, fork rice, cover pan with a folded tea towel or some leaves of kitchen paper, replace lid and leave for 10 minutes, then tip in all the other ingredients and mix very well. It should be really moist and succulent, so, if necessary add some more butter and cream. If using Uncle Ben's rice just follow the cooking instructions on the packet.

FROZEN SALMON

Very few people manage to catch and cook salmon fresh. So if we go on a fishing holiday and are lucky enough to catch a fish, it has to be frozen so that we can get it home before it goes bad. Frozen salmon tends to be dry and can taste of cotton wool if poached in the normal way. In this recipe which was given to me by a fishing friend in Scotland, the milk makes it taste more succulent, and you can feel most people into thinking that they are eating fresh salmon.

4 lbs (1.8kg) frozen salmon
4 pints (2 litres) milk
2 oz (50g) butter
1 onion cut in thick rings
1 carrot cut in 4 lengthwise
1 leek cut in half
1 outer piece of celery
2 bayleaves

1 sprig of thyme
2 good sprigs of parsley
10 black peppercorns
1 teaspoon salt
the thinly peeled rind of 1 lemon

Serves 6–8

Thaw the piece of salmon completely at room temperature, wipe dry and sprinkle inside with a little salt and pepper. Pour the milk into a pan large enough to take the fish, and add all the other ingredients. Bring slowly to the boil and simmer for 5 minutes, then strain into a bowl. Line the pan with a clean tea towel and place the fish on it and fold over. Pour in the flavoured milk, cover and heat up *very slowly* until it is just shivering. Poach for 15 minutes and then pull off the stove and leave to get quite cold. Lift the fish out carefully and remove the skin. Lay on a dish and garnish with thin slices of lemon and cucumber overlapping. Serve with potato salad and Salsa Verde *p. 36*. If you want to serve it hot, leave it to cool slightly in the poaching liquid for 15 minutes then remove the skin and lay on a serving dish. Surround with boiled or new potatoes and serve with Hollandaise Sauce *p. 32*. For a change you can flavour the Hollandaise with 2 oz (50g) finely chopped, blanched sorrel. This 'lemony' flavour goes extremely well with the rather rich salmon. If you want to poach a whole salmon, increase the amount of milk and poach for half-to-three-quarters-of-an-hour, depending on the size of the fish.

SMOKED TROUT FISHCAKES

If you get bored with eating your smoked trout 'straight' or in pâté this recipe makes a nice change.

12 oz (350g) smoked trout, skinned and
boned
8 oz (225g) boiled, mashed potato
1 small onion finely chopped
1 hard-boiled egg coarsely chopped
¼ pint thick Béchamel Sauce (1 oz–25g
plain flour, 1 oz–25g butter, ¼ pint–150ml
milk)
1 dessertspoon chopped parsley
1 teaspoon lemon juice
plain flour for dredging
1 egg beaten well with 1 tablespoon milk
undyed breadcrumbs for coating
salt and pepper
oil for frying

Serves 4–6

Mix together the trout, mashed potato, Béchamel Sauce *p. 27*, onion, hard-boiled egg, parsley, lemon juice and plenty of salt and pepper. Divide into 10–12 cakes and dredge in flour. Now dip each separately in the beaten egg and milk and coat with the breadcrumbs. Fry in oil or a mixture of butter and oil until golden on each side. Serve for breakfast with rashers of crisply fried bacon, or for supper with new potatoes and peas.

SOLE DUGLERÉ

This recipe was given to me by Sylvino Trompetto, the famous Mâitre Chef at the Savoy, on one of the numerous occasions when we lunched there with our friend Johnny Hannay who had started us growing Fraises des Bois. Archie and he were probably drinking a glass of kümmel and after a while, Archie got a bit worried as I hadn't returned so they sent out a search party. I was eventually run to earth in Mâitre Chef Trompetto's private flat beneath the Savoy kitchens quaffing down vintage Moet et Chandon champagne. I don't think they believed me when I said that was all I had been doing!

8 fillets of sole (dover or lemon)
12 peeled and de-seeded tomatoes cut into
tiny dice
1 very finely chopped shallot
1 dessertspoon chopped parsley
1 wine glassful dry white wine
¼ pint (150ml) double cream
either:
1 coffee spoon olive oil if serving COLD
or:
1 oz (25g) unsalt butter if serving HOT
salt and pepper

Grease dish with oil or butter, depending on whether fish is to be eaten cold or hot. Sprinkle in the chopped shallot. Lay fillets of sole on top and cover with diced tomatoes and parsley, season with salt and pepper and pour in the wine. Cover with foil and cook in a moderate oven for 12 minutes at 350°F 175°C Gas Mark 4. When cooked remove the fillets onto a serving dish. Tip the remaining sauce into a small pan and reduce until the liquid all but disappears, then add the cream. Heat but do not allow to boil. Pour over the fillets and serve immediately.

SOLE MEUNIÈRE

The sweet nutty flavour and firm texture of fresh Dover sole makes this, to my mind, a dish fit for a king. You can, of course use Lemon sole or even plaice, but if you want a real treat this is it. It is not necessary to serve a whole fish for each person as it is quite filling and I find two fillets per person ample for a main course and one each as a starter.

2 whole Dover soles skinned and cut into 8
fillets
plain flour for dredging, seasoned with salt
and pepper
4 oz (100g) unsalt butter
good squeeze lemon juice
chopped parsley for garnish
**Serves 4 as a main course Serves 8 as a
starter**

Coat the fillets with the seasoned flour. Heat the butter in a sauté pan until it is foaming. Cook the fillets over a moderate heat until golden on each side. If the butter starts to burn, tip it out and put in some more. Lay the cooked fillets on a warmed flat serving dish. Add a squeeze of lemon juice to the pan juices and a little more butter. Season with salt and pepper. Pour this sauce over the fish and garnish with wedges of lemon and a sprinkle of parsley. New potatoes and spinach go particularly well with this dish. You will find this about as different from the frozen sole you so often get in smart London restaurants as chalk is from cheese.

Pâtes & Terrines

The organization for the 'Ten Acre Shoot' or Tower Hill 1 or 2 is now a military operation, similar in its precision, as Colin Willock describes in his foreword, to Trooping the Colour. After a morning's severe exertion (I have probably been up just before dawn beating in the neighbour's gardens) I miraculously reappear looking civilized, minus twigs in the hair. The table has been laid the night before with all my own and various friends' silver, and every plate, glass and dish in the house. We usually have a fish pâté, four or five smooth pâtés, two or three terrines, a mousse, a hot dish such as Boeuf à la Bourgignonne *p.72* often flanked by at least one secondary hot dish – such as 'Shootable Stag' *p.40*, some salad starters and at least two puddings, (one of which is generally a choccy mousse, by special request from 'the Boss'). All this entails a great deal of work and planning as I am catering for 25–30 people and I usually have a big day of pâté making the previous week. I try and do as much as possible ahead of time and either deep freeze or refrigerate. Most pâtés and terrines benefit from a few days in the fridge anyway. This allows the flavours to develop. On the whole I prefer not to deep freeze terrines as I think they tend to lose their flavour. If you are going to do so it pays to have a heavy hand with the seasoning.

We always argue in this family about which is the most delicious – a smooth pâté or a rough textured terrine. Technically they are both pâtés, but the making of them is totally different. Generally speaking a 'pâté' consists of sautéed liver or meat, seasoned with wine or brandy and pulverised either in a food processor, pestle and mortar (heaven forbid!) or put twice through the fine blade of a mincer. The mixture is then spooned into a china or earthenware dish, allowed to get cold and then covered with a layer of melted lard or butter.

A 'terrine' is made with raw ingredients, either chopped or minced, sometimes marinaded beforehand, mixed with breadcrumbs and egg to bind and cooked in an earthenware 'terrine' (from which it gets its name) in the oven. The usual proportion of fat to lean is one third fat, which can be bacon or pork, to two thirds lean.

People sometmes take fright at the thought of making a terrine, but, in fact, it is merely a rather more exotic form of pork pie without the pastry crust.

CHICKEN LIVER PÂTÉ

This is really a basic recipe to play around with. You can add all kinds of other flavourings if you wish, such as sautéed mushrooms, truffles (if you feel extravagant) or whatever you think might make it different – in fact follow my creed and use your imagination.

Basic recipe

12 oz (350g) chicken livers	small sliver of garlic
4 oz (100g) unsalt butter	½ teaspoon mixed herbs
2 fl oz (60ml) sherry or brandy	salt, and freshly ground black pepper

Serves 8–10

Remove stringy bits from livers and cut up fairly small. Put butter into a sauté or thick frying pan and when foaming throw in the livers. Shake and cook over a brisk heat until cooked but still pink inside. Remove from pan and put into Magimix. Pour sherry or brandy into the pan and bubble for a few seconds. Tip into the Magimix together with all the other ingredients and blend until smooth and creamy. Spoon into a china dish, allow to get cold and then cover with a thin layer of melted butter. Refrigerate for 2 to 3 days. Take out at least 1 hour before you are going to eat it, and serve with hot toast.

CHICKEN LIVER PÂTÉ PAPRIKA or WITH GREEN PEPPERCORNS

Being a game dealer I am lucky enough to have sufficient partridge livers to make them into a 'straight' partridge liver pâté. Unfortunately few people can do this, so I suggest you should use your partridge livers, otherwise just use chicken livers.

8 oz (225g) chicken livers (or partridge livers, or mixture of livers)	1 heaped teaspoon paprika or green pepper-corn purée
4 oz (100g) unsalt butter	3 fl oz (8ml) brandy
1 chopped shallot	¼ teaspoon basil or oregano
¼ pint (150ml) thick double cream	sliver of garlic (optional)
	salt and freshly ground black pepper

Trim the livers and chop roughly. Melt butter in a thick frying pan and sauté livers and shallot until they are cooked but pink inside. Remove from pan. Add brandy, cream, paprika, herbs, garlic and seasoning and bubble for a few seconds. Put everything in the Magimix and blend until really smooth. If you are using the green peppercorn purée do not add it to the pan juices as cooking tends to make it bitter, simply add to the Magimix, and of course omit the paprika altogether. Pour into a dish and allow to get cold. Run a layer of melted butter over the top and decorate with one or two bayleaves and either a pinch of paprika or a couple of dried green peppercorns to denote the type of pâté. Put in the fridge for a few days and use at room temperature.

IRIS'S CHICKEN LIVER PÂTÉ

Iris always said she hated cooking, but this pâté makes me doubt her. It is a deliciously spicy recipe and relies for its flavour on the seasoning, no wine or spirits makes it economical.

1 lb (450g) chicken livers	½ teaspoon grated nutmeg
2 oz (50g) butter for sautéeing	1 pinch ground cloves
6 oz (175g) softened butter	2 teaspoons finely chopped onion
½ teaspoon salt	1 chopped truffle (optional and quite
½ teaspoon ground black pepper	unnecessary, I think)

Beat all the flavourings into the softened butter. Sauté the trimmed and roughly chopped livers in the 2 oz (50g) butter and process in the Magimix until finely ground. Add the seasoned softened butter and the raw chopped onion and blend until really smooth and creamy. Spoon into a china dish and if you have decided to be extravagant, stir in the chopped truffle. Cover, and allow the flavours to develop for at least 24 hours in the fridge before using.

CHOPPED CHICKEN LIVERS

I ate this at a kosher lunch bar in London and thought it so good that I begged the recipe. It should be eaten at room temperature and the consistency should be on the sloppy side, which is why you should try, if possible to use chicken fat. If you can get it, concentrated cooking butter makes a good substitute.

    12 oz (350g) chicken livers
    6 tablespoons chicken fat (or softened
    concentrated cooking butter)
    2 hard-boiled eggs
    3 oz (75g) finely chopped onion
    1 stalk finely chopped celery
    or
    2 oz (50g) finely chopped fennel bulb
    salt and freshly ground black pepper

Sauté the chicken livers in 2 tablespoons chicken fat or butter until they are cooked but still pink inside. Put in the Magimix with the hard-boiled egg yolks and process until finely chopped, but *not smooth*. Tip into a bowl and mix in the rest of the chicken fat or butter and the rest of the ingredients, including the whites of egg which you have chopped roughly. Season – be very generous with the pepper. This does not freeze well as you lose the crunchy texture of the chopped onion and celery or fennel. You can, however freeze the processed chicken livers and add all the other ingredients at the last minute. It makes a change from pâté proper and is nicest served with rye bread or pumpernickel. Be sure and take it out of the fridge at least 2−3 hours before you are going to eat it.

RICH PIGEON PÂTÉ

This is a rich, strongly flavoured pâté and evolved from my first pigeon recipe Pigeon Aspic *p.65*. It took several attempts to get the balance right, as pigeon meat can be rather dry.

    5 pigeons
    1 shallot or ½ small onion finely chopped
    1 oz (25g) smoked streaky bacon, snipped in
    pieces
    4 oz (100g) lard or pork dripping
    4 oz (100g) butter
    2 fl oz (60ml) red wine, sherry or brandy
    ½ teaspoon mixed herbs
    1 clove garlic (optional)
    6 crushed juniper berries
    1 teaspoon redcurrant or rowan jelly
    1 teaspoon made English mustard
    1 scant teaspoon salt
    generous amount freshly ground black
    pepper

Remove breasts from pigeons with a sharp knife and cut into ½″ (2cm) dice. 'Melt' bacon and onion in the butter and lard in a thick frying pan until they are cooked but not brown. Remove from pan and transfer to a bowl. Turn up the heat and sauté the diced pigeon meat until it is cooked but still slightly pink inside then transfer to the bacon and onion. Add wine, sherry or brandy and all seasonings to the pan juices and bubble furiously for a few minutes. Put half the pigeon mixture into the Magimix and process until finely ground, then pour half the liquid in through the top and continue blending until smooth. Repeat operation with the other half. Mix both lots together in a bowl and adjust seasoning if necessary. Put into a large earthenware terrine or several smaller pots and cover. Refrigerate for 2−3 days to release flavours. Best eaten at room temperature and not straight out of the fridge.

TERRINE OF PHEASANT WITH CALVADOS, APPLE AND MUSHROOM

A terrine is more substantial than a pâté, and although you can serve it as a first course I think it is more suited to a cold buffet, or as a main course in the summer with salad.

1 uncooked pheasant
8 oz (225g) chicken livers and the pheasant liver
8 oz (225g) minced pork spare rib (boned)
4 oz (100g) pork fat
8 oz (225g) streaky bacon
½ tin Campbell's condensed consommé
or
5 fl oz (150ml) stock
2 oz (50g) sliced button mushrooms

2 oz (50g) peeled, chopped apple
1 shallot or small onion
1 oz (25g) butter
1 thick slice of crustless white bread
1 egg
2 fl oz (60ml) calvados
½ teaspoon dried thyme
bayleaves
salt and ground black pepper

With a very sharp knife remove as much of the flesh as possible from the pheasant carcass. Cut up roughly and place in the Magimix. Switch on and mince coarsely. Do the same with the pork fat and 2 oz (50g) of the bacon. Chop the shallot or onion and cut up the livers. Put all this in a bowl with thyme, bayleaves, salt, pepper and calvados. Mix well and leave to marinate for 2 hours. Meanwhile soak the bread in the consommé or stock in which you have beaten up the egg. Sauté the apple and mushrooms in the butter for a few minutes. De-rind the bacon and lay the rashers on a board and flatten as much as possible by stroking with the back of a knife. Line an earthenware terrine with all except 2 rashers which you keep for the top. Add the soaked bread and egg mixture and the apple and mushroom to the marinaded pheasant mixture and stir well. Fill the terrine and on top lay the 2 bacon slices, bayleaves and if possible a sprig of thyme. Cover with foil and then the lid. Place in a baking dish and fill with boiling water to come half way up the side of the terrine. Put in a preheated oven 350°F 175°C Gas Mark 4 for 2 hours. Test by inserting a skewer into the centre. If, when you press gently, the juice that oozes out is clear, then it is done. Put a board with a 2 lb (900g) weight on the top and when it is quite cold place in the fridge. If you like you can run a little melted pork fat over the top. Leave for at least 3 days. Either serve in the terrine, or turn it out and cut in slices. Arrange these overlapping on a flat dish and garnish with watercress. Serve with hot french bread.

TERRINE OF PHEASANT AND OLIVES

This is a most unusual and decorative terrine and well repays the trouble of making it.

1 uncooked pheasant
6 oz (175g) pork fat
6 oz (175g) pie veal
2 eggs, well beaten
3 fl oz (80ml) brandy or armagnac
2 finely chopped shallots
½ teaspoon dried thyme

2 oz (50g) stoned green olives
¼ teaspoon ground nutmeg
¼ teaspoon ground cloves
8 oz (225g) pork flare fat
1 sachet aspic
salt and ground black pepper
black and green olives to decorate

With a sharp knife take off all the flesh from the pheasant carcass. Cut the breasts in thin strips and marinate in the brandy or armagnac for 2 hours. Meanwhile, finely chop or mince in the Magimix the rest of the pheasant, the pie veal and the 6 oz (175g) of pork fat, then add the shallot, thyme, spices, egg and the liquor from the marinade and mix thoroughly. Line a terrine with strips of pork flare fat which you have beaten thin. This kind of pork fat is usually only obtainable from a pork butcher and comes in a sheet so it is ideal for this purpose. If you can't get it the best thing to ask for is hard back fat. Fill the terrine with alternate layers of minced mixture and breast fillets, ending up with a layer of mince. Cover with foil and the lid. Put in a preheated oven at 350°F 175°C Gas Mark 4 for 2 hours. Test as in previous recipe. While this is cooking put the carcasses in a saucepan together with a large onion, 2 carrots, 1 leek, a sprig of thyme, 1 bayleaf, 2 cloves, salt and pepper. Cover with water and add a glass of red wine. Simmer for 2 hours, then strain and reduce to 1 pint (575ml) by fast boiling. Dissolve the sachet of aspic in the stock. Take the terrine out of the oven and pour some of the aspic over it. When the terrine has cooled and the aspic has set, remove the specks of fat which will have risen to the top. Run a second layer of aspic over the top and decorate with the black and green olives. Dip these in aspic so that they look nice and shiny. Serve in the terrine. Sit this on a serving dish and garnish with bunches of watercress or sprigs of bayleaves and some clusters of black olives and green olives. It looks most sumptuous.

SMOKED PIGEON PÂTÉ

When I first dreamed up this recipe the only place where you could have bought a smoker would have been a specialist fishing tackle shop at a pretty prohibitive price. Luckily they are now available in Boots Cookshop and are quite inexpensive, so get your nearest and dearest to buy you one for Christmas or birthday, otherwise borrow one from a fishing friend.

This is a true example of the combination of 'sweet & sour'. The honey and lemon are just discernible through the rather strong smoky flavour of the pigeon and give it a certain lightness.

8 pigeon breasts (4 pigeons)
5 rashers of streaky bacon
3 oz (75g) finely chopped shallot
4 oz (100g) unsalted butter
4 fl oz (100 ml) vermouth
1 teaspoon runny honey
2 teaspoons lemon juice
1 teaspoon stem ginger juice or dry ground
ginger
1 tablespoon double cream
¼ teaspoon ground cloves
½ teaspoon mild Dijon mustard
1 pinch dill weed
salt and ground black pepper to taste
Serves 6—8

Sprinkle 1½ tablespoons sawdust over the bottom of the smoker and put in the grid and drip tray. Remove pigeon breasts with a sharp knife, place on the grid and then lay 3 of the rashers on the top. Slide on the lid and put smoke box over the methylated spirits container which has been lit. Leave until it has burned out. Sauté the shallots and remaining bacon in the butter until transparent and transfer to food processor or liquidizer. Cut pigeon breasts into 1″ (2½cm) dice and sauté for a few seconds stirring constantly. Take out and put in the food processor. Pour the juices from the drip tray into the sauté pan with the vermouth, honey, lemon juice, ginger juice (if available), cream and the rest of the seasonings. Increase the heat and bubble furiously for a few seconds. Process the pigeon, bacon and shallots until really finely ground, then pour in the pan juices and blend until really smooth. Put into pot or pots, smooth down and cover with melted butter. Refrigerate for 2 or 3 days to allow the flavour to develop. Serve at room temperature and not straight out of the fridge. Freezes well.

CAROL'S PÂTÉ

During the game season we get inundated with pheasant livers. Try how I might I never managed to make a 'straight' pâté with them – it always turned out to be very bitter. However a friend devised the following recipe by using half pigeon breasts and half pheasant livers. She got full marks from me for using her imagination as, having run out of juniper berries she used gin instead!

4 oz (100g) pigeon breasts
4 oz (100g) pheasant livers
4 oz (100g) butter
2 oz (50g) chopped onion
3 fl oz (80ml) gin
1 teaspoon rowan jelly
½ teaspoon dried thyme
salt and freshly ground black pepper
Serves 4—6

Trim livers and chop roughly, and dice the pigeon breasts. Heat the butter in a frying pan until foaming and sauté the livers, pigeon and onion until cooked but not overdone – still pinkish inside. Put into the Magimix and process until finely ground. Swirl the gin around the pan together with the jelly and seasonings. Pour into the processor and blend well. Spoon into pots and cool. Cover with a layer of melted butter, decorate with bayleaves and juniper berries and refrigerate.

GROUSE PÂTÉ 1

This is a good way of using up old grouse. They are much cheaper to buy and being larger than young birds are more economical.

2 uncooked old grouse	4 juniper berries
8 oz (225g) softened butter	1 teaspoon cranberry sauce or jelly
½ tin Campbell's condensed consommé	4 fl oz (100ml) port or red wine (preferably
4 oz (100g) bacon rashers	the former)
1 small onion	salt and freshly ground black pepper

Serves 8

Place 2 juniper berries and half an onion inside each grouse and season with salt and pepper. Wrap each bird in slices of bacon and spread with softened butter. Pack them into a casserole breast down, with the wine, jelly and consommé and cook in a preheated oven at 300°F 150°C Gas Mark 2 for 2–3 hours. When the birds are tender and the meat is falling off the bones, remove from the casserole. Take all the flesh off the carcasses and cut up roughly. Pour the liquid into a saucepan and reduce over a high heat for a few minutes until it begins to look thick and syrupy. Put everything into the Magimix and blend until really smooth. Spoon into pots and when cool run a layer of melted butter over the top.

GROUSE PÂTÉ 2

This is my favourite grouse pâté recipe as it really does taste of grouse, something which is difficult to achieve with the more usual terrine as all the other flavours tend to intrude.

1 uncooked old grouse	1 teaspoon cranberry jelly
2 oz (50g) butter	3 fl oz (60ml) whisky
2 oz (50g) bacon fat	salt and ground black pepper **Serves 4–6**
1 rasher bacon	

Cut the breasts off the grouse and dice. You can use the carcass for stock. Sauté the grouse and bacon in the bacon fat and butter over a brisk heat until just cooked. Take out and put in the Magimix. Switch on and process until finely ground. Warm the whisky and pour into the sauté pan – light and shake until the flames die out. Pour into the processor together with the jelly and seasoning and blend until smooth. Pot, and when cool put into the fridge. Serve with thin slices of hot toast.

WILD DUCK TERRINE WITH ORANGE

This is a French recipe, which was given to me when I was on holiday. It specifies canard sauvage, or wild duck which means mallard.

1 uncooked mallard	3 fl oz (80ml) orange curaçao or brandy
4 oz (100g) pork fat	¼ teaspoon ground mace
4 oz (100g) lean pork	salt and pepper
2 shallots finely chopped	6 oz (175g) pork flare fat or back fat for
1 egg, well beaten	lining terrine
juice of 1 orange	½ pint (275ml) aspic jelly made with 3
zest of 1 orange	heaped teaspoons aspic dissolved
1 pinch thyme	in ½ pint (275ml) boiling water

Remove the breasts from the duck and cut into long thin slices. Marinate in the orange juice and chosen liqueur for 2 hours. Take the rest of the flesh off the duck carcass and mince with the fat and lean pork. Mix together with the egg, marinade liquor, grated orange zest and seasoning. Line the bottom and sides of a small oval terrine with thin bands of pork flare or back fat. Fill dish with alternate layers of mince and breast fillets, ending up with a layer of mince. Cover tightly with foil and put in a baking dish. Fill half way up the dish with boiling water and place in a preheated oven at 350°F 175°C Gas Mark 4. Cook for 1½ hours or until the juice runs clear when you pierce the mixture with a skewer. When cold pour a layer of aspic jelly over it. When set lay very thin slices of orange down the centre of the dish, slightly overlapping and cover with a final layer of aspic. Serve with hot french bread and Chicory, Orange and Juniper Salad p.85.

FISH PÂTÉS

These are some fish pâtés that I have dreamed up, but there is no end to the variatons of taste and texture that you can achieve by juggling around different ingredients. I am lucky enough to have a small smoker so I smoke all the trout that Archie or I catch, but you can buy smoked trout quite easily, or farmed trout from the fishmonger. Kipper and mackerel also make delicious pâtés. The great joy of this kind of pâté is that it is so quick and easy to make – with a food processor or a blender it is just a matter of a minute or two.

SALMON PÂTÉ

4–6 oz (100–175g) left over cold salmon
1 hard-boiled egg
1 tablespoon mayonnaise
1–2 teaspoons dill or chervil
1 squeeze lemon juice
salt and pepper   Serves 2–4

Blend everything together and adjust seasoning to taste.

SMOKED SALMON PÂTÉ

4 oz (100g) smoked salmon trimmings
2 oz (50g) softened unsalt butter
1 teaspoon dill weed
1 teaspoon lemon juice
salt and cayenne pepper to taste **Serves 4–6**

Put everything in the Magimix and blend until smooth, but don't add the salt until you see how salty the smoked salmon happens to be. Add more lemon juice if you think it necessary.

SMOKED TROUT PÂTÉ

8 oz (225g) smoked trout, skinned and boned
¼ pint (150ml) double cream or homemade or Helman's mayonnaise

2 oz (50g) softened butter
1 teaspoon horseradish sauce
1 tablespoon lemon juice
ground black pepper and salt   Serves 4–6

Put everything in the Magimix or blender and process until smooth and creamy. Taste and adjust seasoning. Serve with granary toast.

SMOKED TROUT AND ALMOND PÂTÉ

8 oz (225g) smoked trout, skinned and boned
⅛ pint (75ml) double cream
4 oz (100g) butter
½ oz (15g) flaked almonds

1 dessertspoon finely chopped parsley
lemon juice to taste (optional)
salt and pepper   Served 6–8

Fry the almonds in the butter until they are golden, then remove to a dish with a slotted spoon. Process the trout with the cream and pour in half the butter through the top of the Magimix. Add lemon juice and salt and pepper to taste. Pour into a bowl and stir in the parsley and half the almonds. Spoon into a china dish and leave in the fridge to get firm. Finally pour over the rest of the butter and decorate with the remaining almonds. The contrast of texture makes this pâté a bit different.

Game

In winter, 'Game' is the name of the game here, which builds up to a crescendo in mid-November when the pheasants start flooding in from the various shoots. I always hope for cold crisp weather – if it is muggy then it's all hands to the deck, including me to 'oven-ready' them.

Sometimes our ancient and rather basic plucking machine breaks down in the middle of making a selection of pâtés for Tower Hill 1 or Tower Hill 2 shoot. Murphy's Law usually arranges for three estates to have been shooting on the same day so that we have more birds than we can cope with. One of the many hats that I wear is that of mechanic, but I can tell you that nothing is more detrimental to a bout of creative cooking than a cri de coeur from one of our ladies with, 'The machine's broken down, Mrs Coats'. So out I have to go and cope with spindles, bearings, plates and fan belts.

But by far the worst disaster that can befall is a telephone call from the only one of our ladies who will gut the birds to say that she is ill. Lucy and I had to 'oven-ready' fifty pheasants and seventy pigeons one Christmas when she had 'flu. But it all adds to the spice of life, and though I grumble I wouldn't have it any other way.

Most game can be hung for up to one week, or more depending on how 'gamey' you like it to taste. But there is no hard and fast rule, and in hot weather, particularly with grouse in August, or partridges in an 'Indian Summer' September, you must watch it or you will have rotten, as opposed to 'hung' birds. Also be sure to keep them in a fly-proof place.

If you are given birds in the feather here is a rough guide as to how you can tell whether they are young or old. I only give the most commonly found varieties.

GROUSE

A young grouse will have a softer beak than an old one, and if you take the beak between finger and thumb the beak will buckle with the weight of the bird. The top of the head will also give a bit when pressed with your thumb. Old birds tend to be heavier and to have more whiskery 'spats'.

PARTRIDGES, English or grey

Look at the flight feather of either sex. If young, it will be pointed, if old, the tip will be rounded. Early in the season the very young birds will have yellow legs, but as the season progresses this is not a sure guide as towards December/January the legs of even a young bird tend to be grey.

PARTRIDGES, French or red—legged

A young bird of either sex will have a white spot at the tip of the flight feather. As time goes on this will become rather more difficult to see and will be just a tiny speck. Old cock birds have very 'knobbly' knees, young ones scarcely at all, though here again, later in the season even a young cock will have quite pronounced 'knobs'.

PHEASANTS

A young cock will have short rounded spurs. An old cock will have long, pointed, curved spurs. Hens are more difficult to tell, but generally the larger and heavier they are the more likely they are to be old.

WOODPIGEON

Not classified as game and therefore has no 'close season' in Great Britain as there is on the Continent. Except by very abstruse and gynaecalogical means there is no way of telling the difference between the sexes, though if you have to gut them yourself, you may find, during the breeding season, eggs in the female. Young pigeons do not have the distinctive white collar of their elders, and really young 'squabs' have downy feathers.

Game freezes extremely well and will keep for up to a year if properly wrapped. Archie and I both think that freezing tenderizes game.

ROASTING GAME

I am constantly being asked how I manage to roast pheasant or French partridge so that it isn't dry. The answer is baste, baste and baste again, and with a few exceptions don't cook them in too hot an oven. A moderate heat for a bit longer pays every time, or so I find. The method for all is the same, heat your butter in the roasting pan until it is foaming, put in the bird(s), coat with the butter and put back in the oven for the requisite time. Baste every 15 minutes. When roasting pheasant I always put a large onion sliced in rings into the pan with the butter and sit the bird(s) on top. This gives a nice colour and flavour to the gravy.

Roasting times:
Pheasant 175°C 350°F Gas Mark 4 1–1½ hours
English partridge 200°C 400°F Gas Mark 6 (10 minutes) then
175°C 350°F Gas Mark 4 (35 minutes)
French partridge 175°C 350°F Gas Mark 4 1 hour

All these should be served with bread sauce and crispings. The sauce that you make should be a 'short sauce' see *p.30* and you can vary the flavourings to your taste. For example you might swill out the roasting pan for your pheasant sauce with cider or stock with a few drops of herb vinegar, and always add a spot of jelly. A few drops of whisky in your grouse sauce will make it quite out of the ordinary.

GROUSE

Grouse is one of the truly British gourmet delights indigenous to this country which you can find nowhere else in the world. It has an unsurpassed 'gamey' flavour, due to the diet of heather buds on which it lives. It can really be said to be a completely wild bird, and fortunately no one has, as yet, started 'farming' it. No embellishments are necessary, and it should be plainly roasted, accompanied by bread sauce, cranberry jelly, 'crispings' and puréed swede or 'neeps'.

About twenty years ago we were staying in a grand Highland hotel. We had been shooting grouse and asked them to cook some of our birds. We sat down to dinner licking our chops in anticipation of delicious juicy birds sitting on squidgy toast. Finally the mind-boggling spectacle appeared of our precious grouse being borne in by the Head Waiter. They were sitting on a bed of limp lettuce and were garnished with pineapple rings impaled on toothpicks. To add insult to injury we had some American friends with us who had never eaten grouse before. We had regaled them with tales of the delights in store, so the whole thing was rather a let-down.

2 young grouse	8–10 oz (225–300g) butter
2 thick slices crustless toast	2 teaspoons cranberry or rowan jelly
2 rashers of streaky bacon	salt and pepper

Salt and pepper the inside of each bird and put a teaspoon of jelly in the body cavity. Melt the butter in a roasting pan in a preheated oven at 400°F 200°C Gas Mark 6 until foaming. Put in the birds, coat well with the butter and put back in the oven for 10 minutes. Now lay a rasher of bacon over the breasts and place each bird on a piece of toast. Cook for 1 hour, basting every 15 minutes. Take out and place on a heated serving dish. Garnish with game chips and serve with bread sauce *p.29*, oatcake crumbled in butter or bacon fat and fried until crisp and a purée of swede *p.84*.

We actually prefer old grouse, and, provided you take care they can perfectly well be roasted. Just follow the same roasting procedure as for young grouse but have the oven temperature at 300°F 150°C Gas Mark 2 and cook for 2–2½ hours, basting frequently, and I mean frequently.

ROAST HONEYED MALLARD DUCK

Unlike domestic duck, wild duck do not have such a thick layer of fat beneath the skin, which tends to make them dry, but we find this recipe a good way of keeping them moist and juicy with a nice crisp skin. Another complaint is that they have a 'fishy' taste. This comes from the preening gland which is situated on the back just where the 'parsons nose' joins the body. If you cut this off the problem will be solved.

2 mallard duck	3 tablespoons runny honey, oil
4 oz (100g) unsalt butter	salt and pepper **Serves 4–6**
1 medium onion	

Rub the ducks with a little oil and salt. Salt and pepper the insides and place a piece of onion in each body cavity. Melt the butter in a pan in a preheated oven at 350°F 175°C Gas Mark 4. Put duck in pan and over each bird dribble a tablespoon of honey. Cook for 1½ hours. Baste frequently for the first hour, then pour on another tablespoon of honey and do not baste again. When done place the ducks on a heated serving dish. Pour the fat out of the pan and swill out with a little sherry or madeira, scraping and stirring. You should end up with a dark, syrupy sauce. Serve with mange-tout peas and Gudrun's Honeyed Potatoes *p.82*.

WILD GOOSE

I must confess that I have not often been faced with the problem of cooking a wild goose and it is now quite a few years since I did so. Desperate wives have rung to say that their loved one has returned from wildfowling grinning from ear to ear, and metaphorically wagging his tail, and bearing the dreaded trophy of a dead Goose! What should be done with it? Should it be buried in the garden for a fortnight, as suggested by one 'old wives' tale'? I don't recommend it. Hang in a cool place for 10 days to a fortnight, then pluck and draw, or (preferably) get the one who shot it to do so! As with Wild Duck *p.58* be sure to cut off the 'parson's nose' and the preening glands. Wash the body cavity well and insert a crust of bread and a large onion stuck with plenty of cloves. Leave for several hours to allow the onion to absorb the fishy smell of the goose. If you wish to make doubly sure, bring a large pan of water to the boil, add 1 tablespoon of salt and 1 teaspoon of bicarbonate of soda. Plunge the bird in for 2 minutes and then remove. Drain well and dry thoroughly and then dredge with flour.

ROAST WILD GOOSE

1 goose prepared as above
1 large onion cut into thick rings
8 oz (225g) unsalt butter
salt and plenty of ground black pepper, or if
you have it Schwartz Lemon Pepper
1 dessertspoon Schwartz Chicken Seasoning

Preheat oven to 300°F 175°C Gas Mark 2. Melt butter and when foaming tip in the onion rings. Dust the inside of the goose liberally with salt and your chosen pepper. Place on top of the onion rings and baste well. Now sprinkle the Chicken Seasoning on the breast and put in the oven on the middle shelf. Roast for at least 2 hours and be sure to baste well every 20 minutes. When done, remove to a serving dish. Pour off most of the fat in the roasting pan and swill round with a wine glassful of red wine or stock and scrape down all the nice brown bits. Pour into a small saucepan, adjust the seasoning and add a teaspoon of redcurrant jelly. Serve with roast potatoes and mashed swede. Another delicious way of roasting wild goose is as follows:—

ROAST WILD GOOSE WITH POTATO & ONION STUFFING

1 wild goose prepared as above
1½ lbs (675g) diced potato
8 oz (225g) finely chopped onion
12 oz (350g) butter
½ teaspoon ground ginger

1 dessertspoon syrup from jar of preserved ginger, or
1 dessertspoon runny honey
salt and plenty of ground black pepper
1 sherry glass sweet sherry

Melt 4 oz (100g) of the butter in a saucepan and then tip in the potatoes and finely chopped onion. Shake well and cover tightly with a lid and cook over a low heat until tender. Add plenty of salt and ground black pepper and the ground ginger and spoon into the body cavity of the goose. Melt the rest of the butter 8 oz (225g) in a roasting pan in a preheated oven 300°F 105°C Gas Mark 2. Put in the bird and baste well. Roast for 2 hours, basting at 20 minute intervals. Half-an-hour before you take it out of the oven cover the breast with the ginger syrup or runny honey. Turn the oven up to 400°F 200°C Gas Mark 6 and allow to crisp. Remove onto a serving dish. Pour off most the fat and swill roasting pan round with the sweet sherry. Adjust seasoning. Serve with new potatoes and braised button onions.

HARE

Hare, like offal, is not everyone's cup of tea. The worst instance of this happened to a neighbour of mine. She cooked a beautifully succulent Civet de Lièvre Royal and as she bore it fragrantly steaming into the dining room her husband said 'Yuk!' or ruder words to that effect and eventually she and her son had to go and eat their dinner in the kitchen, leaving him to dine in solitary state on left−over reheated shepherd's pie! So be quite sure to find out if your guests are 'aficionados' before serving it at a dinner party.

Hare should be hung up by the hind legs with the 'innards' in. The length of time depends on the weather and your preference. If making Jugged Hair or Civet de Lièvre you are supposed to keep the blood, but this rather turns me off so I don't. The following recipe was given to me by a German friend. The entire hare is supposed to be roasted with the head and ears left on, but I can't bear to see any kind of a head, be it woodcock, snipe or even trout, so I decapitate it after skinning or paunching (or better still I get someone else to do it for me)!

ROAST HARE WITH MUSTARD AND BUTTERMILK

1 skinned, beheaded hare
8 oz (225g) unsalt butter
1 tablespoon mild Dijon mustard (or mild, sweet German mustard)
1 tablespoon dry English mustard
1 dessertspoon flour
1 dessertspoon demerara sugar
salt and pepper
1 to 2 pints (575ml−1 litre) buttermilk or milk – you can get buttermilk in most health food stores   **Serves 4−6**

If the hare is very large remove the front and back legs and just roast it as a saddle. Otherwise fix one skewer through the front legs and one through the back legs and tie with string so that the hare will sit nicely on the roasting dish. Place all the ingredients except the buttermilk in the blender or food processor and blend into a paste. Spread evenly over the hare and leave for several hours at room temperature. To cook, Preheat oven to 350°C 175°F Gas Mark 4 and put in the hare in its roasting dish into which you have poured 1 pint (575ml) buttermilk or milk. Cook for 1½ hours basting with the milk, but be careful not to dislodge the jacket of mustard. If it dries out add more milk. Turn the oven up to 400°F 200°C Gas Mark 6 for a further ¼ of an hour. Remove string and skewers and place hare on a serving dish. Scrape the pan down and pour gravy into a sauceboat. Carve as you would a saddle of lamb, and serve with mashed potatoes and red cabbage, *p.83.*

PARTRIDGE NORMANDY STYLE
(Partridge with apple, onion and calvados)

People tend to think that French partridges are dry and tasteless, but the clever French have combined them with their local apples and calvados or 'Applejack' to make them succulent and moist. This is a marvellous way of using old birds and applies equally to French or English partridges which are much cheaper to buy than young ones and 2 old birds will feed 6 people which is economical, though Archie says 'what about the calvados?' My reply is, if you are going to have a treat it is worth spending a bit more, you would have to pay the earth if you had this dish in a restaurant.

2 old French partridges
4 oz (125g) unsalted butter
6 oz (175g) finely chopped onion
1 wine glass calvados or cider (approx 4 fl oz or 100ml)
1 heaped teaspoon cornflour or potato flour
salt and ground black pepper

Melt 2 oz (50g) of the butter in a thick frying pan and sauté the onions and apples until golden, then warm half the calvados, pour into the pan and light. When the flames die out transfer to a cast iron or earthenware casserole. Salt and pepper the insides of the partridges and brown them in the rest of the butter and flame them with the rest of the calvados. Place breast down on the onions and apples. (This is the point at which you add the cider if you have decided against calvados). Put in a preheated oven at 300°F 175°C Gas Mark 2 on the middle shelf for 2−3 hours, or until tender. Remove birds, carve breasts into thin slices and cut off the legs and thighs. Place in a clean casserole. Thicken the apple and onion with 1 teaspoon of potato flour or cornflour mixed with a little water and then pour over the cut up partridge. Serve with mashed potatoes and be sure to have some French bread on hand ready to sop up the delicious sauce.

PHEASANT 'GUIDWIFE'

A wonderful recipe for that 'old stager' with spurs a mile long. It came from an old cook who reigned between the wars in the kitchen of a big house in Herefordshire. It is a great boon as it is even better made the day before your dinner party and slowly reheated, and it freezes exceptionally well. So if like me, at the end of the season you have several 'oldies', it pays to have a session and make them into 'Guidwife' and freeze for future use.

1 old cock pheasant
4 oz (100g) unsalt butter
4–5 large onions, preferably Spanish, peeled and sliced in thick rings
½ pint (275ml) stock or ½ stock cube dissolved in ½ pint (275ml) hot water
½ pint (275ml) red wine

enough fruit chutney p.106 (or mango or peach chutney) to cover the bird generously
beurre manié p.19 or
1 heaped teaspoon potato flour or cornflour mixed with a little water
salt and pepper   **Serves 4–5**

Melt butter in pan and fry onions until golden. Transfer to a casserole. Brown pheasant all over and place on top of the onions. Spread breast and legs of bird with a thick blanket of chutney. Season with plenty of salt and pepper and pour in stock or wine. Place in a preheated oven at 325°F 160°C Gas Mark 3 for 2–3 hours, or until tender. When you take it out of the oven you will find that it has produced a lot of liquid, so thicken this with either beurre manié or a heaped teaspoon of potato flour or cornflour mixed with a little water, until it is the right consistency.

If you have a 'chicken brick' you can do a quick cheat which cuts out the frying, so is good for dieters and is also a time-saver. Lay the sliced onions in the bottom of the 'brick' and then place the pheasant on top. cover with chutney and season. Do not add any liquid. Clap on the top half of the 'brick' and place in a cold oven at 450°F 230°C Gas Mark 7–8 and leave for 1½ hours.

SNIPE

Snipe are a great delicacy and nowadays with farm drainage schemes a considerable rarity. Although we are game dealers and Archie shoots quite a lot, I doubt if I have actually had one to cook for the last two years. On the shoot we have rented for the last twenty-five years or so we have one drive known as 'the Snipe Bog'. In the early days it was an area of boggy fields dotted with reedy tussocks and it was nothing when walking over it to see sixty-odd snipe get up. But alas, no longer. It has now been drained and filled in and is just a boring expanse of cereal crops. Having shot your snipe, and having tossed a coin to see who is going to be lucky enough to eat this delicacy you then have to decide how to cook it and at what stage in the meal it is going to be eaten. My guess is that it should be a savoury, and therefore plainly roasted on a round of fried bread.

ROAST SNIPE

1 snipe
1 thick round bread
4 oz (100g) butter
salt and ground black pepper

squeeze of lemon (optional)
1 Snipe Serves 1 person as a savoury
2 Snipe Serve 1 person as a main course

Pluck the snipe, which won't take more than a second as they are not much bigger than a starling. Then make the great decision:
a) whether to leave on the head and impale the beak through the body,
or
b)whether to leave in the 'trail' or innards.

I don't do either!

Preheat oven to 400°F 200°C Gas Mark 6. Melt 2 oz (50g) of the butter in a small frying pan and fry the round of bread lightly on both sides. Put the rest of the butter in a shallow ovenproof dish in the oven. When it is foaming put in the fried bread with the snipe sitting on top, drench in the foaming butter and cook for 15–20 minutes, basting once again. Serve with a squeeze of lemon and a tiny sprinkle of cayenne. Nothing else is needed. Archie tells me his father would have eaten 5 snipe for breakfast!

WOODCOCK

Woodock, like snipe, is a great delicacy, but rare in places. It is a migratory bird, and, providing the weather is hard a few will be found in boggy places on most shoots. Some are even resident. Like the snipe they are best roast but there are several other good recipes. I think Archie would almost commit murder for a woodcock and if I get a collection in the freezer he goes on nagging until I produce one for him. Archie's father's idea of hanging a woodcock was to leave it 'till it fell off the hook. It is *not* his idea!

ROAST WOODCOCK

1 or more woodcock
1 or more squares of thick toast
4 oz (100g) butter (or as required)
1 or more rashers of streaky bacon
salt and ground black pepper   **Serves 1**

As with snipe, you have to decide whether to leave the 'trail' in or not. Pluck the woodcock and cover the breasts with a rasher of bacon. Preheat oven to 400°F 200°C Gas Mark 6 and melt butter in a roasting pan until foaming. Put in woodcock on its square of toast and baste well. Cook for 25−30 minutes or until the juice which oozes out when you pierce it with a skewer is pink but not bloody. Serve each woodcock on its toast with game chip potatoes and a watercress salad. I think the salad is essential to 'cut across the fats' as my mother used to say. Particularly as woodcock is very rich indeed.

    I sometimes serve woodcock breasts as a savoury. This is simplicity itself.

WOODCOCK SAVOURY

4 breasts of woodcock
4 thin rashers streaky bacon
4 rounds fried bread
rowan jelly
butter for frying
salt and ground black pepper   **Serves 4**

Remove the breasts from the woodcock and cut off the thighs and legs. Wrap each breast in a rasher of bacon and secure with a wooden toothpick. Heat the butter until it is foaming and put in the woodcock breasts. Cook for 3−4 minutes on each side then remove and place on a round of fried bread thinly spread with redcurrant jelly. Season with salt and pepper and serve immediately.

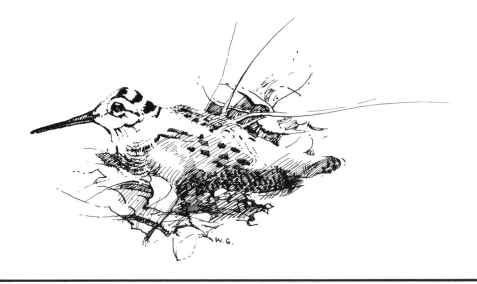

PHEASANT À LA MODE DE BEAUNE

An old favourite which we resurrected not long ago. I had forgotten how delicious it was, but you must be sure to use young birds — preferably hens.

    2 plump young pheasants (hens if possible)
    4 oz (125g) butter
    8 oz (250g) button mushrooms
    2 fl oz (60ml) brandy
    1 heaped teaspoon potato flour or cornflour
    1 pint (575ml) thick double cream
    salt and white pepper   **Serves 6−7**

Preheat the oven to 325°F 160°C Gas Mark 3 and melt the butter in a casserole. Salt and pepper the insides of the birds and put them in the casserole. Spoon over the melted butter, cover and place in the oven. Cook for 1½ hours, or until tender. Be sure to turn the birds every 20 minutes so that they cook evenly. Now add the mushrooms and simmer on top of the stove for 10 minutes. If there is a lot of liquid add the potato flour or cornflour mixed with a little water and stir until it looks smooth. Finally heat the brandy and cream together and pour over the birds. Serve with Pommes Parisiennes *p.82* and tinned Petits Pois.

PHEASANT CREAM

This is an excellent way of using up 'dodgy' pheasants and makes a nice summer dish.

    2 'dodgy' pheasants
    1 onion
    1 carrot
    1 celery stalk
    1 chicken stock cube
    1 pint (575ml) water
    1 wine glass white wine
    pinch mixed herbs
    1½ oz (40g) butter
    1½ oz (40g) plain flour
    ½ pint (275ml) double cream whipped
    2 oz (50g) roughly processed cooked ham
    2 oz (50g) sliced button mushrooms lightly
    sautéed in a little butter
    ½ oz (15g) gelatine dissolved in a little hot
    stock
    salt and pepper
    pinch curry powder

Pepper and salt the insides of the pheasants and place in a saucepan breast side down with the onion, carrot, celery, stock cube, herbs, white wine and water to cover. Cook very gently on top of the stove, the water should be barely moving. Test for tenderness after 2 hours. If done, leave to cool in liquid.
   For the sauce: melt the butter over a low heat, add flour and cook for a few minutes. Pour in 1 pint (575ml) pheasant stock and whisk well. Cook over a very low heat, stirring every so often until it has reduced to ½ pint (275ml). Remove meat from birds, discarding skin and bones and any lead shot. Place in Magimix with the sauce. Switch on and process, but do not let it get too smooth. Pour into a bowl and add ham and mushrooms. Adjust seasoning and allow to cool. Add melted gelatine and, when almost set fold in the whipped cream. Pour into a soufflé dish or a ring mould. Serve with cold rice into which you have stirred a tablespoon of mango chutney and a tablespoon of finely chopped spring onions. If you have used a ring mould, turn the pheasant cream out onto a dish and fill the centre with the rice. A crunchy Fennel or Celery Salad p .... makes a good contrast to the texture of this recipe.

VENISON

A few years ago if you had wished to serve venison at a dinner party you would have found it difficult to get hold of except perhaps from somewhere like Harrods, and certainly it would never have been available outside London. Nowadays, though not commonplace, you can find it in the bigger supermarkets and the better butcher will be able to get some for you even if he doesn't have any in stock. Red deer, roe, fallow and sika are the four varieties. Roe and sika are, to my mind the most delicious and don't need all the marinading and attention that is required if you are suddenly landed (as I have been) with a haunch of red deer venison from an affectionate relative in Scotland.

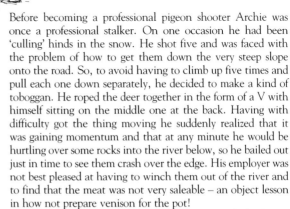

Before becoming a professional pigeon shooter Archie was once a professional stalker. On one occasion he had been 'culling' hinds in the snow. He shot five and was faced with the problem of how to get them down the very steep slope onto the road. So, to avoid having to climb up five times and pull each one down separately, he decided to make a kind of toboggan. He roped the deer together in the form of a V with himself sitting on the middle one at the back. Having with difficulty got the thing moving he suddenly realized that it was gaining momentum and that at any minute he would be hurtling over some rocks into the river below, so he bailed out just in time to see them crash over the edge. His employer was not best pleased at having to winch them out of the river and to find that the meat was not very saleable – an object lesson in how not prepare venison for the pot!

The recipe I give is for red deer, as roe deer and sika do not need to be marinaded, and you can treat them just like lamb.

ROAST HAUNCH OF VENISON

1 piece of red deer haunch weighing 6−8 lbs (2.75− 3.65kg)
2 tablespoons redcurrant or rowan jelly
8 oz (225g) softened butter
2 very finely chopped shallots
1 dessertspoon concentrated tomato purée
2 oz sliced button mushrooms
½ oz (15g) dried wild mushrooms simmered in ½ pint (275ml) stock
1 glass red wine
1 good pinch dried thyme
For the marinade:
4 tablespoons oil
1 tablespoon wine vinegar
salt and ground black pepper

Hang the piece of haunch in a cool fly-proof place for 7 to 10 days, depending on the weather, having first wiped it dry and rubbed it well with ground ginger and black pepper. 24 hours before you are going to cook it, wipe clean with a damp cloth. Put in a large bowl or dish and spoon over the marinade mixture. Keep turning it over so that the marinade does its tenderizing work properly.

Preheat oven to 400°F 200°C Gas Mark 6. Dab the haunch dry with kitchen paper and spread with the softened butter, redcurrant jelly and chopped shallots. Sprinkle on the thyme, pepper and salt and encase loosely in silver foil. Leave enough space for air and steam to circulate inside the parcel and place on a baking dish in the oven. Leave for 20 minutes then reduce oven heat to 325°F 160°C Gas Mark 3 and continue cooking for 3½ to 4 hours. Remove the foil and transfer the meat to a serving dish. Carefully tip the liquid which will have gathered inside the foil, into a saucepan, add the tomato purée, the wine and the wild mushrooms in their stock and reduce rapidly to a rich syrupy sauce. If you wish to thicken it add ½ teaspoon potato flour or cornflour mixed with a little water. Serve with mashed potatoes and Purée of Swedes *p.84* or Kohl Rabi *p.83*.

Pigeon

If I was to take a bet on the first remark that people make when they hear that I am married to a professional pigeon shooter I should be very rich. They always say 'I suppose you make a lot of pigeon pie.' This is what Archie and I call the 'pigeon pie mentality'. Although pies can be delicious there are so many other interesting ways of cooking them. On the continent, particularly in France they are really considered a delicacy and people will go to a lot of trouble when cooking them.

Another thing people often say in a jocular kind of way is 'Don't you die if you eat pigeon for a fortnight?' No so long ago I had to write an article on pigeon cookery and bombarded the family with a different recipe every day for a week – we are still very much alive and kicking, so that's another myth exploded.

The great secret when cooking pigeon is that you must either cook it very quickly for a short time, or for a very long time as slowly as possible.

PIGEON ASPIC

I think it is only fitting that I should start this section with the first recipe I ever invented. This was about thirty years ago, before the advent of food processors, and even a liquidizer was pretty rare. So if you were one of the less fortunate you had to wrestle with a hand operated mincer which made cooking a bit of a struggle.

This is a delicious dish for hot weather and is not expensive to make.

6−8 pigeons
2 oz (50g) fat bacon
2 oz (50g) butter
2 hard-boiled eggs (optional)
1 tablespoon red wine, sherry or brandy
1 clove garlic (optional)
1 teaspoon redcurrant jelly
1 teaspoon made mustard
3 heaped teaspoons aspic dissolved in ½ pint

(275ml) boiling water OR ½ oz (15g) gelatine dissolved in ½ pint (275ml) hot stock (or 1 chicken stock cube dissolved in ½ pint – 275ml hot water) ½ teaspoon mixed herbs salt and plenty of ground black pepper
1 x 8″ (20cm) round or oblong earthenware terrine
a few bayleaves for decoration *or* an orange

Serves 6–8

Remove pigeon breasts. Cut into 1″ (3cm) dice, snip bacon into pieces or cut into dice. Melt butter in a thick frying pan and sauté bacon, but do not allow to brown. Remove to a dish. Sauté pigeon until cooked but still faintly pink inside, remove with a slotted spoon and add to the bacon. Make the aspic or gelatine and stock, reserve ⅓ cup for the final decoration. Add wine, garlic, mustard, redcurrant jelly and herbs to the pan juices and swirl round for a few seconds. Now place all the ingredients except for the 2 hard−boiled eggs in the Magimix or blender or put the bacon and pigeon through the fine plates of a mincer twice and then beat in the other ingredients. Cover the bottom of the terrine with 1″ (3cm) layer of the pigeon mixture lay the eggs lengthwise down the centre and cover with the rest of the mixture. Smooth down, decorate with bayleaves and cover with cling film and leave to get cold, then place in refrigerator. Finally, pour over the rest of the aspic. As a variation you can add a little orange juice to the aspic and instead of bayleaves decorate with thinly cut, overlapping slices of orange. This makes a delicious summer dish served as a main course with salad. If you are going to freeze it you must omit the hard−boiled eggs as the whites go black if you put them in the deep freeze.

PIGEON PUDDING

In February or March when your particular 'pigeon shooter' has been killing a lot of birds on the newly sown corn or the oil seed rape you may be a bit stuck for ideas as to how to use them up. A pigeon pudding is one answer as you need at least 10 pigeons to make it, but it is also delicious, filling and warming.

10 pigeons
1 small onion finely chopped
1 teaspoon rowan jelly
1 rasher streaky bacon snipped into small pieces
¼ teaspoon mixed herbs
1 bayleaf
plain flour seasoned with salt and pepper
2 fl oz (60ml) red wine
Suet Crust
8 oz (225g) self raising flour
4 oz (100g) suet
½ teaspoon salt
¼ pint (150ml) water   **Serves 4—6**

Remove the pigeon breasts and cut into ½″ (2cm) dice, then roll in the seasoned flour. To make the suet crust, sieve the flour and salt into a bowl. Mix in the suet with a knife and then add water until it makes a soft dough. Turn out onto a floured board and reserve ⅓ for the lid. Roll in the flour and then roll out lightly until it is large enough to line a 1 ½ pint (850ml) pudding basin, leaving a little hanging over the rim. Fill with the pigeon, onion, bacon and jelly, stick a bayleaf in the middle and sprinkle with the herbs. Pour in the wine and enough stock to come just below the level of the pigeon. Moisten the edge of the suet crust with water and cover with the remainder which you have rolled out to fit. Pinch together and trim off any overhanging pieces. Cover with foil, but leave enough room for the crust to rise. Steam for 4 hours. Serve with mashed potatoes and swedes.

SALMI OF PIGEON

This is a nice easy recipe as you can roast the pigeons ahead of time, and then prepare the salmi so that all you have to do is to heat it through just before you want to eat.

3 whole roast pigeon
4 oz (100g) butter
2 oz (50g) flour
1 pint (575ml) stock made from the pigeon carcasses
4 fl oz (100ml) port or red wine
2 finely chopped shallots
4 oz (100g) button mushrooms
1 dessertspoon redcurrant jelly
1 dessertspoon concentrated tomato purée
1 pinch dried thyme
salt and pepper   **Serves 4—6**

Preheat the oven to 350°F 175°C Gas Mark 4. Melt 2 oz (50g) of the butter in a pan and when foaming put in the pigeons which you have seasoned with salt and pepper. Baste well and cook for 1 hour. Take out of the oven and allow to get quite cold. Cut off the breasts and the thighs and legs (the birds should be underdone and pink) and put the carcasses into a saucepan. Add 1 onion stuck with cloves, 2 carrots sliced lengthways, a stick of celery, a pinch of mixed herbs, pepper and salt and cover with 2 pints of water. Simmer gently until the liquid has reduced by half. Melt the rest of the butter in a saucepan, add the finely chopped shallots and the mushrooms and cook for a few minutes. Sprinkle in the flour and stir well then pour in the stock slowly, stirring constantly until it thickens, then add the redcurrant jelly, tomato purée, port or red wine, herbs and seasoning. If it looks anaemic add a few drops of gravy browning. Cook over a low heat for 10 minutes and then pour over the pigeon breasts and legs. Cover and heat through gently.

PIGEON AND TANGERINE CASSEROLE

This is an unusually flavoured dish and freezes well. I don't possess one, but I think this recipe would cook very well in a slow cook pot, and, of course for those of you with an Aga, just stick it in the low oven and forget it for a few hours.

4–6 pigeons
4–6 rashers of bacon
lard or dripping for frying
4–6 tangerines or small oranges
2 shallots peeled and cut up
1 medium onion peeled and cut up

1 level tablespoon plain flour
¼ lb (100g) small button mushrooms
2 fl oz (60ml) sherry or maderia
½ teaspoon mixed herbs
salt and freshly ground black pepper

Serves 6–8

Stuff birds with tangerine or orange. Brown them in hot fat and remove to a casserole. Chop shallots and onion and cut up the bacon. Sauté in the remaining fat until pale gold but not brown, add the mushrooms and cook for a few minutes. Sprinkle in the flour, then add the sherry or madeira. Cook until it thickens and then pour over the pigeons. Add the salt, pepper and mixed herbs. Cook in a low oven 300°F 150°C Gas Mark 2 for 2–3 hours.

PIGEON TERRINE

A very useful terrine. It is nice as a main course in the summer, or in winter as part of a packed shooting lunch when you are asked to take your own.

10 pigeon breasts
4 oz (100g) pigs liver
4 oz (100g) minced pork
4 oz (100g) pork fat minced
8 rashers smoked streaky bacon
2 shallots finely chopped
2 fl oz (60ml) sloe gin

¼ teaspoon dried thyme
¼ teaspoon ground cloves
1 egg beaten up in 2 fl oz (60ml) milk
1 thick slice of white bread without the crust
bayleaves to decorate
salt and ground black pepper   Serves 6–8

Cut 5 of the pigeon breasts lengthways into thin slices, lay in a dish and marinade in the sloe gin for 2 hours. Chop or mince the liver, the remaining 5 pigeon breasts and 2 of the bacon rashers and mix together with the pork, port fat, shallots, thyme, cloves, the bread slice which you have soaked in the egg and milk, and the marinade liquor. Line an earthenware terrine with 6 of the bacon slices which, you have flattened and stretched with the back of a knife. Put in ½ the mixture, then lay the pigeon slices on top and end up with the rest of the mixture. Place the remaining 2 bacon slices on top and decorate with the bayleaves. Cover tightly with foil and stand in a baking dish. Fill with boiling water to come half way up the side of the terrine and place in a preheated oven at 350°F 175°C Gas Mark 4 for 2 hours, or until the juice runs clear when you stick in a skewer. Remove from oven, place a 2 lb (900g) weight on top and when cool place in the fridge for 2 or 3 days to allow the flavours to develop. Serve with hot toast as a starter or with a salad as a main course.

SAUTÉED PIGEON BREASTS

This is a real 'quickie', but it must be done at the very last minute. Don't even let it sit whilst you are eating your first course.

3 pigeons
1 tablespoon seasoned plain flour
2 oz (50g) unsalt butter
1 dessertspoon redcurrant jelly
1 tablespoon red wine

1 tablespoon cream
salt and pepper

Serves 2–3

Remove breasts from pigeons and cut into thin strips lengthwise. Roll in the seasoned flour and sauté in the butter for *no more than 1 minute* on each side. Remove to a serving dish. Now add the redcurrant jelly, wine and cream to the sauté pan and allow to bubble for a few seconds. Adjust seasoning and pour into a sauceboat. Serve with mashed potato.

ESCALOPE OF PIGEON BREAST STUFFED WITH CREAM CHEESE AND GARLIC

This was a case of 'great minds think alike'. We had a surfeit of pigeon breasts and I had been complaining to Lucy that I needed a new recipe. She came down for the weekend and started to tell me about an idea she had had for stuffing pigeon breasts with cream cheese. I said nothing, but when dinner came produced the following recipe – we both agreed that it must have been telepathic communication.

4 pigeon
8 teaspoons Rondelé,
Tartare or Sainsbury's cream cheese with
garlic and herbs
2 eggs beaten up in 2 tablespoons milk
plain flour for dredging
undyed breadcrumbs
4 oz (100g) unsalted butter for frying
Serves 4–6

Cut off the pigeon breasts. (Use the carcasses for stock). Insert a sharp knife along the side of the breast and make as big a pocket as possible. Take a teaspoon of your chosen cheese and insert with a rounded knife, spreading as evenly as possible. Dredge with flour. Dip the floured breasts in the egg and milk mixture and then coat with the breadcrumbs. Do this a second time just along the opening of the pocket to ensure that the cheese does not escape during cooking. You can do all this in the morning and lay the prepared breasts on a dish and put in the fridge until the evening. You can also freeze them, but they *must* be completely unthawed before before you cook them.

To cook. Heat the butter in a sauté or thick frying pan until it begins to foam. Now drop in the breasts and cook for *no more* than THREE MINUTES on each side. They should be faintly pink and tender. If cooked any longer they will be like wedges of rubber. Equally good cold, see *p. 86*.

BREAST OF YOUNG PIGEON IN CREAM SAUCE

In the autumn there should be plenty of young pigeons. They are easily distinguished by their lack of white collar and 'downy' feathers. This is a quick and easy dish to prepare.

4 young pigeons
2 oz (50g) unsalt butter
¼ pint (150ml) double cream
4 very finely chopped shallots
1 teaspoon teriyaki sauce
(available from good delicatessen or
grocers)
1 teaspoon demerara sugar
Schwartz garlic pepper
Schwartz seasoned salt
4 slices thick toast (optional)   **Serves 4**

Cut off the breasts. Melt the butter in a thick frying pan until it is foaming, then put in the pigeon breasts and the chopped shallots. Cook for *no more* than THREE MINUTES on each side. Transfer onto the pieces of toast which you have laid in a shallow fireproof dish. Pour the cream, teriyaki sauce, garlic pepper and seasoned salt into the frying pan and bubble for a few seconds, then dribble it over the pigeon breasts. Place under a very hot grill for 2 or 3 seconds until the sauce begins to brown and then serve immediately. Omit the toast if you like a lot of sauce, as it soaks up all the juice. If you don't have garlic pepper, use ground black pepper and garlic powder or crushed fresh garlic, and plain salt. As this is a very rich dish, serve with mashed potatoes and a crisp salad – iceberg lettuce or chicory is nice, and a Vinaigrette Dressing *p. 36*.

PRUE'S PIGEON PIE

The gauntlet was thrown down so I had to accept the challenge. A friend said to me "Over the years you and Archie have both said and written time and again that you wanted to change the British Housewife's attitude to pigeon – what you called the 'Pigeon Pie Mentality'. I challenge you to make a mouth−watering pigeon pie." What could I do but accept? I must admit that I have had to literally eat my words – so to speak, and the following recipes have passed the test of my severest critics – Archie and Lucy, and of course my challenger.

I have noticed at various times when I have come across recipes for pigeon pie that they nearly all contained stewing steak. This seemed to me highly derogatory to the pigeon, as though people thought it hadn't got enough flavour on its own, but on further reflection I decided that, unlike us with our limitless supply of pigeon people were using steak to pad out their recipes. I may be wrong, but I am trying to take the charitable view. Anyway, as far as I am concerned it's pigeon, pigeon all the way and the main ingredient for *my* two pies is pigeon.

HOT PIGEON PIE

    1½ lbs (675g) pigeon breasts (8 pigeons)
    8 oz (225g) finely chopped onion
    2 oz (50g) finely chopped carrot
    4 oz (100g) pork sausage meat
    1½ oz (40g) smoked streaky bacon
    2 tablespoons Country Herb Stuffing (or any
    good packet stuffing with herbs) soaked in 1
    tablespoon of boiling water
    2 teaspoons rowan jelly
    ¾ pint (425ml) stock or ¾ pint (425ml)
    boiling water in which you have dissolved 1
    chicken stock cube
    ¼ pint (150ml) red wine
    seasoned flour for dredging
    salt and freshly ground black pepper and 2
    bayleaves

Serves 6− 9

Take a sharp knife and remove the breasts from the pigeons. Place the carcasses in a saucepan of water with a carrot, an onion a bouquet garni and 2 bayleaves. Simmer for 2 hours or until you have a nice rich stock. If you can't be bothered to do this do as suggested above and substitute water and a chicken stock cube. Cut the pigeon breasts into ½" (2cm) dice and roll in the flour together with the onion and carrot. Place in a casserole and cover with ¾ pint (425ml) stock and ¼ pint (150ml) red wine. Add more stock if the liquid does not completely cover the pigeon. Put on the lid and place in the oven which you have preheated to 250°F 140°C Gas Mark 1. Cook for 3 hours and then test for tenderness. The pigeon should literally melt in the mouth. If it doesn't, cook for a further half−an−hour. Transfer to a pie dish, taste and adjust seasoning if necessary. Cover with cling film or foil and allow to get completely cold. Make the sausage meat and the stuffing into balls the size of a marble and dot them over the pie meat. Roll each of the bacon rashers and cut in half and do likewise.

SHORTCRUST PASTRY

    6 oz (175g) plain flour
    4 oz (100g) unsalt butter
    1−2 tablespoons water
    1 pinch salt

Sieve the flour and salt into the food processor. Cut the butter into 1" dice and add to the flour. Switch on and process for 15 seconds. Add 1 tablespoon water and switch on. Process until it forms a ball. If it doesn't, add a little more water, but be wary or you will have a sticky mess. Remove and wrap in cling film. Rest in the fridge for an hour. Then take out and roll out lightly as thin as possible. Cover the pie and decorate nicely with pastry leaves. Brush with egg yolk beaten with a little water. Place in a preheated oven 425°F 200°C Gas Mark 7 for 12 minutes then turn oven down to 350°F 175°C Gas Mark 4 for another 25 minutes. Remove from the oven and add a little hot stock. Serve with mashed potatoes and swedes or glazed baby turnips.

COLD PIGEON PIE

This recipe is nice enough to serve at a dinner party or as part of a party buffet. When I produced it I asked my guests to guess what it was. None of them got it right, though you would have thought it would have been easy – the clues being right under their noses so to speak, with Archie being a 'Professional Pigeon Shooter'. The majority thought it was grouse. The secret of its succulence lies in the rich jellied stock. I'm afraid this is a fairly extravagant recipe as it uses 2½ lbs (1.1kg) pigeon breasts which equals 12 pigeons!

2½ lbs (1.1kg) pigeon breasts
(or 12 pigeons)
1 large onion stuck with 4 cloves
1 strip of lemon peel
¾ pint (425ml) stock made from the pigeon carcasses (procedure as in above recipe)
½ oz (15g) dried wild mushrooms (obtainable from any Health Food Store)
3 hard−boiled eggs
1 chicken stock cube

4 oz (100g) fresh button mushrooms
2 teaspoons redcurrant jelly
½ oz (15g) gelatine dissolved in 2 fl oz (60ml) sherry
1 tablespoon aspic
1 shake lemon pepper
1 shake garlic pepper
1 good pinch mixed herbs
salt and ground black pepper if necessary

Serves 6−8

Cut the pigeon breasts up as in previous recipe. Put in a casserole together with the onion, dried wild mushrooms, redcurrant jelly, mixed herbs and chicken stock cube. Cover with the stock and cook in a preheated oven at 250°F 140°C Gas Mark 1 for 3 hours or until absolutely tender. Remove the onion and put the pigeon in a pie dish with stock to come half way up the dish. Allow to get quite cold and then lay the button mushrooms and quartered hard−boiled eggs over the top.

Make Shortcrust pastry as per previous recipe and cover the pie. Place in a preheated oven at 425°F 220°C Gas Mark 7 for 12 minutes, then turn down to 350°F 175°C Gas Mark 4 for 30 minutes or until the pie is golden brown. Whilst the pie is cooking melt the gelatine in the sherry and the tablespoon of aspic in ¼ pint (150ml) boiling stock. Mix together. Take the pie out of the oven and make a funnel with some cardboard, (I use a postcard). Pour in the aspic/gelatine mixture very carefully until you can see it right up to the top of your pigeon mixture. Don't let it overlfow or your pastry will go soggy. Serve with new potatoes sprinkled with chopped dill.

Meat & Poultry Offal

BEEF

Beef is not worth eating unless it has been well hung. To achieve this result you have to find a good butcher, which is like trying to locate a crock of gold. Several years ago I went into a big chain store butcher and asked the old man in a straw boater who was serving if I could have a sirloin on the bone which had been well hung for 2 weeks. 'Madam,' he said, 'I have been here for three years and you are the first customer who has asked me for a piece of well hung meat'.

Don't be deterred if your well hung piece of meat looks a bit purple on the outside – so much the better. It should also be sightly marbled with fat which will make the meat more tender. This is virtually impossible to obtain as everyone is so cholesterol conscious that farmers are producing nothing but very lean meat. As a family, we tend to go for meat on the bone as it has more flavour. This is our favourite recipe – fore-rib is less expensive than sirloin and has, we think more flavour.

ROAST FORE-RIB OF BEEF WITH YORKSHIRE PUDDING

6–8 lbs (2.7–3.6kg) fore-rib of beef
8 oz (225g) softened butter
1 tablespoon dry mustard

1 dessertspoon Worcester sauce
1 wine glassful of red wine
salt and ground black pepper   **Serves 6–8**

Make a paste of the softened butter, mustard, Worcester sauce, salt and pepper and spread it on both sides of the joint. Preheat the oven to 400°F 200°C Gas Mark 6. Put the joint on a rack in the roasting pan and place in the oven. Cook for 15 minutes to the pound (rare) 20 minutes (medium), or 25 to 30 minutes (well done) and 15 minutes over. Baste well every 20 minutes. When cooked, remove onto serving dish and allow to rest for 30 minutes in a warm place as this will make it easier to carve. Meanwhile, pour off most of the fat and scrape off the brown bits. Swirl out with wine, then pour into a small pan. Reduce by fast boiling until thick and syrupy and adjust seasoning. You may find you have to add a teaspoon of brown sugar to counteract any acidity from the wine.

Serve with 'Bag of Nails Potatoes', *p.82*, Yorkshire Pudding, below, and Horseradish Sauce *p.30*. Beef, unlike lamb, should be carved in very thin slices, about ⅛″ (¼cm) thick.

YORKSHIRE PUDDING

4 oz (100g) plain flour
¼ teaspoon salt
2 eggs

¼ pint (150ml) milk
1 tablespoon dripping, oil or butter

Sieve flour and salt into Magimix. Switch on and break in the eggs, then add the milk. Process until smooth and creamy. Put 1 tablespoon of dripping, oil or butter in an 8″ (20cm) cake tin on the top shelf of the oven until very hot. Pour in the batter – it should sizzle and bubble round the edge of the tin. Cook for 35 to 40 minutes. Move it to the bottom of the oven if it starts to burn. Everyone has their own idea, but I think it should be crisp round the outside and slightly soggy in the middle.

BOEUF À LA BOURGIGNONNE

This Burgundian Beef Stew at its best is a gourmet's delight and is as far removed from the fatty, gristly stew you find in tins as it is possible to be. I usually have it once a year for the hot dish at one of my shoot lunches and the smell emanating from the kitchen whilst it is cooking makes the gastric juices work overtime! I usually cook a gallon of it in my monster Elizabeth David earthenware casserole, which comes rather expensive on the wine and brandy, but here is a recipe for more modest quantities which will feed 6–8 people. Like all casseroles it is even better when reheated.

Some recipes tell you to marinade the meat, but it is a bore and makes it very difficult to get the beef dry enough to fry.

4 lbs (1.8kg) chuck steak, trimmed of fat and cut into 1″ (2cm) cubes
flour to dredge, seasoned with pepper and mixed herbs
8 oz (225g) green fat bacon cut in dice
¼ pint (150ml) oil
4 oz (100g) unsalt butter
¼ pint (150ml) cheap cooking brandy
4 carrots diced
2 whites of leek cut into rounds
8 oz (225g) coarsely cut up onion
1 stick celery, diced
2 fat cloves garlic

1 split pig's trotter (optional)
1 bottle heavy red wine, preferably burgundy
1 teaspoon mixed herbs
2 bayleaves
1 dessertspoon demerara sugar
2 oz beurre manié *p. 19*
Garnish
8 oz (225g) very small button mushrooms trimmed but not peeled
24 small onions, Paris Silverskin if possible or small pickling onions
salt and ground black pepper   **Serves 6–8**

Melt half the oil and butter and sauté the diced bacon until brown but not crisp, then transfer to an earthenware or cast iron casserole. Now sauté the cubes of beef and cook until brown. Warm brandy, pour over meat and light. Shake until flames die out and put into the casserole with the brandy. Melt the rest of the oil and butter and cook the chopped onion, garlic, carrots, leek and celery until coloured. Add to casserole, together with mixed herbs, bayleaves and demerara sugar and season well. Pour on the burgundy and top up with stock or water to cover, if necessary. Lay pig's trotter on top, this will enrich the sauce considerably. Place in a preheated oven at 275°F 140°C Gas Mark 1 for 3 hours. Take out of the oven and skim off all the fat. Complete this operation by blotting with squares of kitchen paper until all the fat has been absorbed (even if it takes a whole roll of paper!) Add the beurre manié and stir until it has all been absorbed and replace casserole in the oven for a further hour or more if it seems necessary. When done remove trotter and have another session with the kitchen paper. Just before serving add the mushrooms and onions which you have cooked in a little butter and decorate with triangles of fried bread and lots of chopped parsley. Serve with plain boiled or new potatoes or hot french bread and a crisp green salad.

As with all casseroles this dish is better made ahead of time and reheated – the flavours will then have had time to permeate. It freezes well, but it pays to freeze it at the first fat skimming stage and continue the further cooking after unthawing. If you complete cooking and then freeze it, when you come to heat it up it may become over cooked and stringy.

SCOTCH MINCE COLLOPS

This was invariably the main dish at Archie's old home in Scotland when they had a shooting lunch, and is a far cry from the nasty grey stuff which I remember at school. Always buy best lean ground beef, or get your butcher to mince it for you. When Lucy was at Edinburgh University she went to buy some mince and, mindful of the fatty stuff sold under the guise of mince in the south, she asked the butcher for some 'best lean mince'. He was highly offended and said his mince was '*all* best and lean'.

2 lbs (900g) best lean mince
1 large onion, finely chopped
1 tablespoon pinhead or medium oatmeal
(Health Food stores stock this)
½ beef stock cube

1 pinch mixed herbs
2–3 drops gravy browning
salt and plenty of ground black pepper
1 dessertspoon oil for frying   **Serves 6**

Heat oil in a thick frying pan until smoking. Tip in the mince and scrape and turn with a fork until it is all sealed and there are no raw looking lumps. Turn heat down and add onion, herbs, stock cube and 2 or 3 drops of gravy browning. Season to taste and sprinkle in the oatmeal. Transfer to a thick earthenware or cast iron casserole with a tight fitting lid. Place in a very low oven 300°F 150°C Gas Mark 2 for 2−3 hours. Look at it occasionally and give it a stir. The end result should be a rich, savoury, shiny looking mixture. The oatmeal will have absorbed any moisture so it should not be swimming in greasy liquid. Garnish with tiny triangles of toast and serve with mashed potatoes and Purée of Swede p.84.

LAMB

There is nothing more delectable than a succulent leg of English lamb, or better still hill lamb which is leaner and has a nuttier flavour. It should be just faintly pink inside and with a golden brown crispy skin. When choosing your joint, pick one with nice white pearly fat, this denotes quality and youth. In Scotland ask for a 'Gigot' – the same word in French, so presumably a relic of the 'Auld Alliance' between Scotland and France.

ROAST LEG OF LAMB

1 leg of lamb weighing 4–5 lbs (1.8–2.2kg)
4 oz (100g) butter and 1 tablespoon oil
1 onion cut in thick rings
1 tablespoon redcurrant jelly
Schwartz Lamb Seasoning
3 or 4 sprigs of fresh rosemary or a sprinkle of
dried
garlic (optional) or garlic pepper
salt and freshly ground black pepper
¼ pint (150ml) wine or stock (real or made
with a stock cube)

Preheat oven to 350°F 150°C Gas Mark 4. Make small slits in the outer skin and stick the lamb with the sprigs of rosemary and as many slivers of garlic as you wish. Rub with oil and sprinkle with Lamb Seasoning, pepper and salt and spread with the redcurrant jelly. If you don't want to use real garlic just use a sprinkle of garlic powder or garlic pepper. Melt the butter in the roasting pan until it is foaming. Place the joint on a grid and spread the onion rings out underneath so that they will catch the drips from the joint. Put in the oven and give a preliminary baste. Cook for 1½ to 2 hours, basting frequently. When done, remove to a serving dish to rest in a warm place. Pour most of the fat out of the pan and add the wine or stock and allow to bubble on top of the stove, scraping well. The onions will have caramelized, making the gravy a nice dark colour. Strain into a small pan, swill the roasting pan out again with a little more stock and scrape off any remaining brown bits and pour into the gravy. Heat through and reduce if necessary. Finally adjust the seasoning. Serve with new potatoes and peas – Sainsbury's frozen petits Pois are very good. I prefer new to roast potatoes as lamb tends to be rather rich. Lamb should be carved in fairly generous slices about ¼″ (¾cm) thick.

BOILED LEG OF MUTTON WITH CAPER SAUCE

Lamb officially becomes mutton when it has reached the age of one year or more and is generally a ewe which has lambed. Proper mutton is extremely difficult to find which is a pity as I think it has more flavour, so you may have to make do with an October lamb. If not, buy the largest lamb joint you can find and the chances are that it will be more mature. If the size, and price put you off, buy a half.

1 leg of lamb (mutton)
4 to 6 medium onions
3 carrots cut in half lengthways
4 leeks
1 stick celery
2 turnips *or*
1 small swede
1 dessertspoon demerara sugar
salt and ground black pepper   **Serves 6–8**

Bring a pan of water to the boil and put in the lamb or mutton. Allow to come slowly back to the boil, skim and continue to simmer very slowly for ½ hour skimming every time the scum comes to the surface. Cut the leeks and celery into 4″ (10cm) lengths and the turnips or swede into pieces but leave the onions whole. Put in with the lamb and add the sugar and plenty of salt and pepper. Cover tightly and simmer very gently for 1½ to 2 hours for lamb and 3 hours for mutton. The liquid should just shiver. If your hobs are too fierce place a simmering mat beneath the pan or cook in a casserole in the oven at 300°F 150°C Gas mark 2 for 3 to 4 hours (depending on whether it is lamb or mutton). When cooked, remove onto a dish and keep warm while you make the sauce, (See *p.27*). If Caper Sauce does not appeal to you, then make a rich Onion Sauce *p.28*. Serve the vegetables with which it was cooked, and plain boiled potatoes.

VEAL

Stewed or casseroled veal can be a bit bland and tasteless so why not try the following recipe with sorrel or chervil which gives it a little 'bite'. If you have difficulty in getting loin of veal, try using loin of pork it is almost as good.

VEAL OR PORK LOIN WITH SORREL SAUCE

2–2½ lbs (900g–1.1kg) loin of veal or pork
4 oz (100g) unsalt butter
4 shallots
1 sprig of thyme
1 sprig of tarragon
1 sprig of parsley
1 bayleaf

1 carrot cut in two
½ pint (275ml) stock
½ pint (275ml) white wine
4–6 oz (100–175g) sorrel
½ pint (275ml) thick double cream
2 egg yolks
plenty of salt and ground black pepper

Brown the veal or pork loin in the butter with the shallots and carrot and transfer to a cast iron or eartenware casserole. Add the herbs, stock and white wine and cover tightly. Cook in a preheated oven for 2 hours at 300°F 150°C Gas Mark 2. Remove meat to a serving dish and keep warm. Strain the cooking liquid into a saucepan and reduce by rapid boiling to ¼ pint (150ml). Chop the sorrel roughly and cook in 1 oz (25g) butter over a very low heat for about 10 minutes, stirring constantly. Pour in the reduced cooking liquid and process in the Magimix or blender and return to the pan. Now add the cream and egg yolks and stir until it begins to thicken, but do not allow to boil or it will curdle.

Serve in a sauceboat separately or pour over the loin. Mashed potatoes are all you need to accompany this delicate dish. Failing sorrel you could use purée of spinach with a good squeeze of lemon juice, or Chervil which is also delicious. Make the sauce in the same way.

OXTAIL STEW AND DUMPLINGS

This rich and succulent dish is one of the most economical I know. The only trouble is that unless you have an old fashioned butcher it is rather like going to buy a wool dressing gown in the spring, you will be told it is the wrong time of year. My family love it and a certain painter friend, who has a distinct interest in this book, always sniffs hopefully when coming into the house as it is his favourite dish. Archie always says mine is not so good as the one made by Cousin Constance which is simmered for hours and hours in the low oven of her Aga, but hope springs eternal and every time I make it I hope to receive the accolade of 'as good as Cousin Constance's'. Last time I made it I got 2 stars or 'almost as good as'!

OXTAIL STEW

2 small oxtails
2 large onions stuck with cloves
2 carrots
1 leek
3 fat cloves garlic
1 teaspoon mixed herbs
4 bayleaves

1 tablespoon redcurrant jelly
2 tablespoons concentrated tomato purée
1 bottle red wine
1 oz (25g) dried wild mushrooms soaked in
½ pint (275ml) water
seasoned flour for dredging   Serves 6–8

Trim as much of the fat as possible from the pieces of oxtail and coat in the seasoned flour and then brown in the heated oil. Transfer to a casserole with a slotted spoon and brown the carrots, leeks and onions in the remaining fat. Add to the oxtail together with the jelly, tomato purée, mixed herbs and bayleaves. Pour on the red wine, the mushrooms and their water into which you have crumbled the stock cube. Place the casserole on the bottom shelf of the oven which you have preheated to 250°F 140°C Gas Mark 1 and cook for 5 hours or until the meat is falling off the bones. Skim well and finish blotting off the fat with kitchen paper until there is none left. Remove onions and carrots. Serve with plain boiled potatoes, carrots and small glazed onions. You can also serve it with suet dumplings. The stew is definitely best made the day before and reheated for 1 hour at 300°F 150°C Gas Mark 2.

Here is my father's recipe for suet dumplings. I can't think why he gave it to me as he didn't cook but it's in his handwriting and it works.

TREAD'S DUMPLING RECIPE

2 cups plain flour
2 tablespoons minced butcher's suet
3 teaspoons baking powder
1 teaspoon salt
1 cup milk

Mix well and drop dessertspoonsful into really fast boiling salted water. Leave for 15 minutes without lifting lid. Remember they swell so do use a really large saucepan.

Any stew left over can be converted into Oxtail Soup, see *p. 23*.

FOREHOCK OF GAMMON VIRGINIAN STYLE

If you don't want to go to the expense of buying a whole or half gammon, buy a whole forehock from your butcher, or, better still from your local pork butcher or pie shop. One end may be a bit fatty, but it will be most succulent and there will be plenty of lean for the Jack Sprats. It is a rather difficult joint to carve, but once you get the hang of it you will find it very economical, and it looks very nice as part of a summer buffet.

1 whole smoked forehock weighing about 6−8 lbs (2.7−3.6kg)	½ cup mango chutney juice or wine vinegar cloves
1½ cups demerara sugar	1 15½ oz (450g) can pineapple rings
1 tablespoon dry mustard	**Serves 10−12**

Soak the forehock overnight in plenty of water. Place in a large pan and cover with fresh water. Bring slowly to the boil and simmer very slowly – the water should barely move. Allow approximately 20 minutes to the lb, but test with a skewer. Leave to get cold in the cooking water. Preheat oven to 400°F 200°C Gas Mark 6. While it is heating up skin the joint, and score the fat in a diamond pattern. Stick in a clove at each intersection, and spread on the sugar, mustard and chutney juice/vinegar which you have mixed together. Place on a grid in the baking dish in the oven for 45 minutes, basting several times. 20 minutes before it finishes cooking lay the pineapple slices round the pan. When done, remove joint onto a serving dish and garnish with the pineapple slices. Now tip in the pineapple juice and bubble pan on top of the stove, scraping and stirring. Pour into a bowl and allow to get cold, then skim off the fat. Tip into a sauceboat and serve with the forehock either hot or cold.

CHICKEN

What can I say about chickens except that they ain't what they used to be. The best you can do is to try and find somewhere like a farm or a farm shop which sells fresh, free range hormone and antibiotic free birds. Failing this the quality in any of the big supermarket is pretty good if you go for fresh and not frozen. But the flavour will never be the same as the real farm-reared cockerels I used to buy, preferably a maran – one of those gentlemen in a grey and black striped suit whose breed originated in France, and whose female counterparts lay those unbelievably dark brown speckled eggs.

ROAST CHICKEN WITH LEMON, ONION & PARSLEY STUFFING

1 chicken weighing 4 lbs (1.8kg)
8 oz (225g) unsalt butter
8 oz (225g) finely chopped onion or shallot
8 oz (225g) fresh breadcrumbs
1 tablespoon chopped parsley

juice & rind of ½ lemon
1 egg yolk
Schwartz Chicken Seasoning
salt and freshly ground black pepper

Serves 6−8

Melt half the butter in a pan and fry half the chopped onion until cooked but not coloured and mix together with the breadcrumbs, parsley, juice and rind of lemon and egg yolk. Season with salt and pepper and stuff the chicken. If you wish to vary the stuffing you can add a little chopped sautéed bacon and/or sliced mushrooms. Preheat the oven to 350°F 175°C Gas Mark 5 and melt the rest of the butter in the roasting pan until foaming. Sprinkle in the remainder of the chopped onion and place the chicken on top. Baste well and sprinkle liberally with the Chicken Seasoning. Cook for 1½ hours, basting frequently. Remove onto serving dish to rest for 10 minutes or so in a warm place. Add ¼ chicken stock cube and ⅛ pint (75ml) water and allow to bubble for a few seconds. Pour into a sauceboat and this will make just the sort of gravy you get in France. It took me a great many years to work out how they achieved the wonderful 'sauce' which came with any roast fowl and I finally tumbled to the fact that they always used unsalted butter. You can, if you wish add a little top of the milk or thin cream. Instead of serving roast potatoes, try Pommes Parisienne *p.82*.

DUCK

The sort of duck you can buy nowadays from most supermarkets are usually mass produced Aylesbury ducklings. By chance I tumbled on what I think are the best brand. I had housed some goods for a friend, on behalf of a friend of his. When eventually they were collected, a huge van drove in to pick them up with 'Cherry Valley Ducklings' written all over it. I said to the driver jokingly, 'Well I think that after a year of housing these boxes your boss might at least let me have a duck!' I never thought any more about it until two days later a voucher came by post entitling me to six ducks – I have never bought any other brand since. The other breed of duck to look for is a Muscovy, rather larger than an Aylesbury and with darker slightly 'gamey' flesh, or the French 'Canette de Barbarie'. These are pricey but delectable.

CRISPY DUCK ROASTED WITH SALT

1 3–4 lb duck
Coarse sea salt
oil
1 onion cut in thick rings
pepper
2 fl oz (60ml) madeira or sweet sherry
Serves 2–4

Preheat oven to 375°F 190°C Gas Mark 5. Prick duck skin all over, salt and pepper inside body cavity, rub all over with oil and sprinkle generously with salt. Pour 1 tablespoon of oil into roasting pan, put in onion rings and place duck on a rack or trivet on top. Place in oven and roast for 1 ½ hours. Do not baste or you will prevent the skin from becoming crisp. It will in any case baste itself with the layer of fat beneath the skin. Turn the heat up to 400°F 200°C Gas mark 6 for last 10 minutes. Remove bird onto a serving dish, pour off the fat and swill the roasting pan round with the madeira or sherry and strain into a sauce boat. Serve with new potatoes and tinned petits pois.

TURKEY

Why is it that the mention of Turkey at Christmastime strikes fear into most cooks (even if they don't admit it). No one thinks twice about roasting a chicken or even a turkey at any other time of the year but at Christmas it seems to be different and we worry if it is going to be dry, undercooked or overcooked.

The great secret is to try and get your act together well beforehand, with as many things as possible in the deep freeze. Unfortunately the turkey cannot actually be stuffed until Christmas Eve at the earliest, and better still Christmas morning as the warm stuffing provides a haven for the breeding of Salmonella bacteria. You can, if really pushed, make the stuffing ahead of time and either freeze it or put in the fridge the day before. If, like me, you are addicted to chestnut stuffing, I hate to tell you that there is no short cut to the laborious chore of peeling the chestnuts unless you have a microwave, (which I don't). If you do, simply cut a cross on the top of the chestnuts and pop them in for 1 minute. They will then slip out of their skins quite easily. I have tried using tinned 'marrons' and dried chestnuts and both are disgusting.

Try and choose a fresh turkey if possible, even if you freeze it yourself. A hen is generally more tender than a cock, though if you want a monster the biggest hen won't weigh much more than 16 lbs (7.2kg). If you can, get a Broad Breasted Bronze. They are the real thing and taste just like the ones we used to rear ourselves when we first came to live here. Anyway, what's wrong with turkey at other times of the year? Cold turkey on its own or with chaudfroid sauce p.34 is a super summer dish.

ROAST TURKEY WITH MUSHROOM, APPLE, ONION & CALVADOS STUFFING

1 turkey weighing 14 to 16 lbs
1 lb (450g) unsalt butter
Serves 10–12

Mushroom, onion and apple stuffing
6 oz (175g) finely chopped onion
6 oz (175g) sliced button mushrooms
4 oz (100g) finely chopped peeled & cored apple
8 oz (225g) breadcrumbs
2 egg yolks
2–3 fl oz calvados

Sausagemeat stuffing
1 lb (450g) pork sausagemeat
good pinch mixed herbs

Chestnut stuffing
1 lb (450g) good quality chestnuts
stock to moisten
salt and pepper
1 pint stock made from the giblets
1 lb (450g) pork chipolatas
12 rashers streaky bacon
1 dessertspoon cranberry jelly
plenty of salt and ground black pepper

It helps if you make the giblets into stock as soon as you get your turkey, then you can freeze it and it will be to hand when you want to start operations. Do not include the liver as it will make the stock bitter, keep it and use it in a pâté later. First of all loosen the skin over the breast of the bird and put in a layer of butter – about 8 oz (225g) so that the breast will be deliciously moist. Try and spread it as evenly as possible. Now sauté the chopped onion, apple and mushrooms in the rest of the butter. When it is just beginning to colour, warm the calvados and pour it over and light. Shake until the flames die out and mix into the breadcrumbs together with the egg yolks. Stuff the turkey with this mixture, leaving enough room at the rear end for the sausagemeat which you have seasoned well with the mixed herbs and ground black pepper. Cut the tops off the chestnuts, cover with water and bring to the boil. Cool slightly and peel with a sharp knife. Put the peeled chestnuts into a small pan with ½ (275ml) pint of the giblet stock and season with salt and pepper. Simmer until tender and mushy, then squash with a potato masher. Insert into the neck cavity and fold the flap of neck skin over and sew or tie up. Truss the bird and place in a preheated oven at 350°F (175°C) Gas Mark 4 and cook for 20 minutes to the pound. Baste every half-an-hour. 1 hour before cooking is complete put in the bacon rolls and chipolatas which you have threaded onto skewers. If the bird is getting burnt cover the breast with a square of foil. 10 minutes before you take it out of the oven remove foil and turn oven up to 400°F (200°C) Gas Mark 6. Take out and place on warmed carving dish surrounded by the bacon rolls and chipolatas. Leave to rest in a warm place while you make the gravy and dish up the vegetables. Pour off as much of the fat as you possibly can or suck it off with a bulb baster. Let it bubble on top of the stove and scrape down the pan. Pour into a saucepan, add the cranberry jelly and reduce to about 1 pint (575ml). Taste and see if it needs any more seasoning, it probably won't because all the delicious flavours of the stuffings will have seeped into it. Serve with a big jorum of bread sauce, *p.29* plenty of 'Bag of Nails' potatoes *p.82*, purée of swedes *p.30* and brussels sprouts or whichever vegetable you prefer.

The vital 'one hour before cooking is complete' may leave you in need of a 'cooks nip'. You will be much helped by a good slug of 'Archie's Bloody Mary' *p.108* – you can always blame any subsequent disasters on its potency.

CALVES LIVER SANTÉ

We very rarely eat out, but when we do we go to the lovely Italian family restaurant of Mr and Mrs Santé, Franco & Santé, Hampstead House, Basingstoke. There we get a marvellous welcome and delicious food. We try to resist the heavenly pasta and go straight on to the Calves Liver with Sage.

4 slices of calves liver cut *paper thin* (very important)
2 oz (50g) butter
1 tablespoon oil
4 shallots
12 leaves fresh sage (or dried)
salt and freshly ground black pepper

Serves 4

Heat the oil in a thick frying pan, then add the butter. When this is foaming put in the slices of liver and cook for 2 minutes on each side. Transfer to a warm dish. Now throw in the chopped shallots and the sage leaves and fry quickly until brown, then pour everything over the liver and serve immediately. If necessary you must leave your guests after the first course and cook the liver, as it must not be kept waiting. Serve with sautéed potatoes, courgettes and spinach.

CALVES SWEETBREAD IN EGG AND BREADCRUMB

This is more appreciated on the continent than it is over here. Beware having it a dinner party without first asking your guests if they like it. Once when we were staying with Archie's cousin on our way north they arranged a family dinner party. We sat down eight to dinner and when the main course of sweetbreads arrived everyone except Bettys (cousin's wife) and I looked as if they were going to be sick! Eventually she and I scoffed the lot and the other six had to make do with a few rather meagre slices of ham destined for the morrow's shooting sandwiches!

When Lucy and I decided we wanted to have some sweetbreads we did not know how to cook them. Finally we discovered that you have to soak them in cold water for 2 hours, then place in a pan, cover with cold water and bring to the boil, cook for 5 minutes, drain and place in cold water. Then skin them and place beneath a board with about 4 lbs (1.8kg) weight on top. Do all this preparation in the morning and they will then be ready to cook in the evening.

1 calves sweetbread, blanched, skinned and flattened
1 egg beaten up in a tablespoon milk
flour for dredging
breadcrumbs for coating
2 oz (50g) butter
2 tablespoons oil

Serves 2—4

Cut the prepared sweetbread into pieces 2″ x 4″ (5 x 10cm) dredge in flour and coat in egg and breadcrumbs. Heat oil and butter in a sauté pan and fry the sweetbread pieces until golden on both sides. Lift out and drain on kitchen paper. Arrange on a serving dish with a garnish of button mushrooms which you have sautéed in the remaining fat. Serve with wedges of lemon, a green salad and new potatoes.

Vegetables & Salads

Compared to even five years ago there is such a variety of salad ingredients and unusual vegetables available that you never need get bored with cooking or eating the same old thing day after day. Lots of things can be grown in your garden if you live in the country, Thompson & Morgan in particular have a wonderful selection of seeds so do be adventurous and try some of the more exotic varieties. Amongst those I particularly like are Asparagus Peas, a vetch like plant of spreading habit with a ridged seed pod which, if steamed for five minutes and served with melted butter, is quite delicious. Romanesco, a pyramidical pale green broccoli, Kundulus carrot (otherwise known as the Windowsill Carrot) a very quick growing carrot with round roots a little larger than a marble, and our very favourite potato the Pink Fir Apple Salad Potato. These are shaped like a long pink sausage with knobs. They should be boiled or steamed in their skins which should be peeled off after they have been cooked. You then slice the potatoes in rounds and use them in potato salad or sauté them. They remain in perfect condition like new potatoes until January or February. In fact, Sainsbury's sold them last year, so someone must have heard the good news. Kohl rabi is another little known vegetable of the turnip family. It is very easy to grow, and provided you use it when young it has a very delicate flavour, but is not so woody as turnip.

There are a lot of vegetable and salad recipes available, so I shall just give some of my favourites. Here are a few general hints that may be useful.

BRASSICAS, BEANS AND PEAS

Cabbage, calabrese, brussels sprouts, peas, broad beans, runner beans and french beans should be cooked in plenty of fast boiling, salted water for as short a time as possible, anything from 5 to 10 minutes. Keep testing by taking a bite, they should be 'al dente' i.e. slightly crunchy. When they have reached this stage, drain them well, and add plenty of butter and shake them around in the pan. French beans are improved by a drop of oil with the butter.

SPINACH

This does not come into quite the same category as the above. It should be washed in several lots of water to remove any grit and dirt and then drained and put in a saucepan with a knob of butter. Cover with a lid and place pan over a very low heat. After a few minutes take the lid off and turn the spinach over so that the bottom leaves are at the top. Now continue cooking for about 15 to 20 minutes, shaking every so often. You will find that it has shrunk by at least half and that there is a lot of liquid. Take the lid off and continue to cook stirring occasionally until most of the liquid has evaporated. Now it is ready to put either in your liquidizer or food processor with some cream, or to serve 'en branche'.

ROOT VEGETABLES

Always cook these in a minimum of water with the lid on over a very low heat. I usually cut them into cubes and put them in a pan with a knob of butter, a pinch of sugar and about 2 tablespoons of water. By root vegetables I mean swedes, turnips, parsnips and kohl rabi. Carrots should however be cooked in boiling salted water, drained and then finished off in butter and sugar.

'BAG OF NAILS' POTATOES

This is not a recipe from the notorious night club of the war and post—war years, but from a pub of the same name in Victoria where Archie and I used to meet clandestinely for lunch. We considered the menu ambrosial. Don't laugh when I tell you that it was generally Spam fritters (there was still rationing) and these gorgeous roast potatoes meltingly crisp on the outside and floury within. Success in making them is partly due to the variety of potato – they must be floury and not waxy, and should measure about 5″ (12½cm) x 3″ (7½cm) when peeled. They should then be sliced in half lengthways to produce a shallow oval disk. Cook in boiling salted water and drain while they are still just firm, and beginning to look floury on the outside. Now heat 1″ (3cm) of oil or dripping in a shallow roasting pan and put in the potatoes. Sprinkle with salt and score lightly with a fork and then baste well. Preheat oven to 350°F 175°C Gas Mark 4 and put in potatoes on the bottom shelf and roast for 1½ hours. Then drain off the oil and transfer pan to top of the oven for another 1 hour. If the meat or poultry you are cooking has to be roasted at a lower temperature than this, put the potatoes at the top of the oven and when you have taken the meat out to rest, turn the oven up to 400°F 200°C Gas Mark 6 for 15 to 20 minutes.

GUDRUN'S HONEYED POTATOES

My sister-in-raw is Swedish and this is her special potato dish. It is particularly good with roast wild duck and pork.

> 1½ lbs (675g) peeled potatoes
> 2 oz (50g) butter
> medium oatmeal (for sprinkling)
> 1 tablespoon runny honey or golden syrup

Cook the potatoes whole then cut in four lengthways and then in thick chunks. Melt the butter in a frying pan, put in the potatoes and sauté for a few minutes. Sprinkle with a little oatmeal and dribble the honey all over them. Keep turning them in the butter and honey until they become golden. Sprinkle with salt and pepper and serve immediately.

POMMES PARISIENNES

When new potatoes are out of season and you are bored with all the other ways of cooking them, these make a change, but you must have very large potatoes and a kitchen gadget which makes potato balls or melon balls.

> 4 extra large potatoes – size approx 5″
> (12½cm) x 3″ (7½cm)
> 2 oz (50g) butter
> 2 tablespoons oil

Peel the potatoes and, with the larger end of the gadget, winkle out as many balls as possible. Do not wash. Heat the butter and oil in a sauté pan with a lid. Turn down the heat and sauté the potatoes for 10 minutes shaking the pan the whole time so that they don't stick to the bottom. If you don't want to use them immediately cover and leave. Finally take off lid, turn up the heat, keep shaking the pan and cook until they are golden all over – about 10 minutes. Serve immediately.

CURLY KALE

This is known mainly as an ingredient of Scotch Broth, but properly cooked it can be used as a substitute for spinach. Discard any tatty or old coarse—looking leaves and remove the stalk or midrib from those remaining. Chop up roughly and cook in fast boiling, salted water until tender, about 8 minutes. Drain well and press out any moisture. Place in the Magimix with 1 oz (25g) butter and 1 tablespoon of cream and process until you have a smooth purée. Add a scrape of nutmeg if you feel like it and use as you would spinach.

If you want to use it as a starter – just cook in boiling salted water, drain and serve with melted butter.

KOHL RABI

Kohl rabi is very easy to grow and is delicious to eat. Sainsbury's sell it, so, if you don't live in the country and see them on the shelf 'have a go' and try them.

    4 or 5 small kohl rabi peeled and cut in
    quarters
    1 oz (25g) butter
    1 teaspoon sugar
    1 small pinch dill weed
    salt and pepper

Steam for 20 minutes to half–an–hour, or until tender, then toss in butter and sugar, and finally add the seasonings.

PUMPKIN

As I have said elsewhere in this book, this is a much under–rated vegetable, and in November, after 'Hallowe'en' it makes a nice change from cabbage and root vegetables.

    2 lbs (900g) pumpkin peeled and diced
    6 oz (150g) onion
    1 dessertspoon demerara sugar
    1 clove garlic
    2 oz (50g) butter
    1 pinch mixed herbs
    salt and plenty of ground black pepper

Chop onion and garlic very finely. Melt butter in a saucepan and add the onion and garlic. Cook with the lid on over a low heat until transparent and then put in the pumpkin, sugar and seasonings. Stir and turn occasionally and cook slowly until tender and all the liquid has evaporated.

RED CABBAGE

One of my favourite winter vegetables – almost a meal in itself. Goes well with pork and game.

    1½ lbs (675g) red cabbage
    1 rasher bacon
    1 apple
    1 onion
    1 dessertspoon demerara sugar
    ½ teaspoon black peppercorns
    1 pinch cumin seeds (optional)
    1 pinch dill seeds (optional)
    ¼ pint (150ml) wine vinegar
    1 tablespoon bacon fat (or oil if no fat)

Slice the cabbage thinly, cut up the bacon and chop the apple and onion coarsely. Melt the fat in a saucepan over a low heat, put in the bacon and cook for 2 minutes, then add the cabbage, apple and onion. Stir and turn well to coat with the fat or oil, then add the vinegar and seasonings. Cover tightly and cook over a low heat for 1 hour, stirring occasionally. Add a little more vinegar if it begins to dry out. It is done when all the liquid has evaporated and the cabbage is tender. Adjust the seasoning and add more sugar if it seems at all sour.

SPRING GREENS

These are what I yearn for at the end of the winter when I am sick of colourless cabbage and root vegetables and the now inevitable iceberg lettuce. Don't overcook them into a soggy dark green mess. Take a little trouble and you have a vegetable fit for a king.

> 2–3 heads of spring greens
> 2 oz (25g) butter
> salt and pepper

Remove the tough outside leaves, though early on you will probably be able to use everything. Cut off any hard stalk. Wash and chop across the greens starting at the top and working towards the stalk, this ensures you don't get any stringy bits when you put it in the Magimix. Throw the greens into a pan of fast boiling, salted water and cook until tender but still slighly crunchy, about 5 minutes. Drain well, tip into Magimix with the butter and process in short sharp burst until coarsely chopped but not puréed. If you don't want to process them, just serve as they are with the butter.

PURÉE OF SWEDES

A 'must' with roast grouse, and goes well with all kinds of game, poultry and particularly lamb. Archie complains that what we get in the South is nothing like the 'neep' or sheep turnip he remembers from his youth in Ayrshire. I always puzzled over the Scottish word 'neep' until I came to the conclusion that it must be a diminutive of turnip i.e. tur'neep'. The other Scottish word is 'purry' presumably another relic of the 'auld Alliance' being derived from the French purée. The best I can do is to try and give him swedes from Cornwall when they are in season. Grown in the red Cornish soil, they have a lovely deep orange colour when cooked. The following recipe is a far cry from the watery, stringy swede served up in most schools.

> 1½ lbs (675g) swede cut into 1" (2½cm) dice
> 4 tablespoons water
> 1 dessertspoon demerara sugar
> 1 oz (25g) butter
>
> 1 tablespoon cream
> nutmeg
> salt and ground black pepper

Cook the diced swede in a covered pan with the water, sugar and salt over a very low heat until tender – about half–an–hour, but be careful not to let it burn dry. When cooked, drain (save the liquid for gravy) and tip into the liquidizer or food processor. Turn on and whizz until creamy. Now add the butter, cream, ground black pepper, more salt if necessary and 2 or 3 scrapes of nutmeg, (or a pinch of powdered nutmeg). Process for another few seconds and spoon into a serving dish.

AVOCADO, QUAILS EGGS, LETTUCE AND BACON SALAD

A nice contrast in textures. The rather bland avocadoes are set off by the crisp lettuce and crunchy bacon.

> 3 ripe avocado pears
> 1 kos lettuce (failing this use an iceberg lettuce)
> 4 rashers smoked, streaky bacon grilled until crisp
> 6 hard-boiled quails eggs, peeled
> Coats Salad Dressing p. 34.
>
> 1 teaspoon chopped capers
> 2 chopped cocktail gherkins
> 1 chopped shallot
> 1 dessertspoon chopped parsley   **Serves 6**

Discard any coarse looking lettuce leaves and arrange the remainder around the edge of a shallow dish or bowl. Peel and halve the avocadoes and place them in the middle and in the centre of each put a quails egg. To the Coats Salad Dressing add the capers, gherkins, chopped shallot and chopped parsley and dribble it over each of the avocado pears. Finally, crumble the bacon and sprinkle it on the salad. Serve with hot garlic bread.

CELERI REMOULADE

Celeriac Salad with Remoulade Sauce
This is the recipe to go with the Remoulade Sauce on p.35

    1 celeriac weighing about 1 lb (450g)
    amount of Remoulade Sauce 2 on p.35

Peel the celeriac and cut in julienne strips, or if you have an attachment for your Magimix which makes matchstick potatoes use this. Plunge into boiling salted water for 30 seconds then rinse under the cold tap and drain. Dab dry with a tea towel. Put into a bowl and mix well with the Remoulade Sauce. Best left overnight to absorb the flavour. Can be served as a starter, as part of an hors d'oeuvres or as a salad to accompany cold meat – particularly pork.

CHICKEN SALAD

This is the salad for which the Cooked Chicken Salad Dressing p.34 is primarily designed. It makes an effort free, easy to eat main course for a summer buffet, and you can always vary the ingredients to suit what is available, or what you feel like.

    1 lb (450g) cold cooked chicken
    8 oz (225g) cold cooked ham
    2 lbs (900g) cold cooked potato
    1 head celery
    Cold Cooked Salad Dressing as per recipe p.34
    1 teaspoon chopped chives
    1 teaspoon chopped parsley
    sprigs of watercress to garnish
    paprika to garnish
    salt and ground black pepper   **Serves 8–10**

Cut the chicken, ham and potato into 1" (3cm) cubes and put in a large bowl. Scrape the strings off the celery stalks and chop it all up coarsely and add to the bowl. Pour over the cooked salad dressing and mix thoroughly adding salt and ground black pepper if necessary. Arrange in a shallow mound on a flat dish and sprinkle over the chives, parsley and a little paprika to give a contrast of colour. Garnish with sprigs of watercress. Serve with Tomato Rings p.88 filled with cold cooked peas.

CHICORY AND ORANGE SALAD

A fresh tasting, crisp salad which goes well with duck.

    2 sticks of chicory
    1 orange peeled and sliced
    6 crushed juniper berries
    Dressing
    1 teaspoon Dijon mustard
    1 teaspoon sugar
    1 dessertspoon orange juice
    1 teaspoon lemon juice
    4 tablespoons sunflower oil
    salt and pepper   **Serves 2–4**

Slice the chicory in rounds. Peel the orange with a knife so that there is no white pith and cut in segments. Sprinkle on the crushed juniper berries and pour on the well mixed dressing.

SALAD OF COLD STUFFED ESCALOPES OF PIGEON BREAST

This is an excellent way of using up any pigeon escalopes you may have left over after eating them hot.

4 cold cooked stuffed Escalopes of Pigeon
Breast *p.68*
1 stick chicory
or
2 hearts of celery
or
1 fennel bulb
4 dessertspoons vinaigrette sauce, made with
lemon juice
4 coffee spoons redcurrant jelly   **Serves 4**

Cook the pigeon breasts as per the recipe on *p.68* and either allow them to get cold or use ones that are left over. Take each breast and cut in paper thin slices diagonally across. Arrange in overlapping slices on 4 plates. Decorate with thin rounds of your chosen salad over which you dribble a dessertspoon of vinaigrette sauce *p.36*. Garnish each escalope with a coffee spoonful of redcurrant jelly.

Fennel

FENNEL SALAD

This salad goes particularly well with cold smoked trout and it can be used to accompany Gravadlax p.44, instead of Gravadlax Mustard and Dill Sauce p.35.

    2 fat fennel bulbs
    3 tablespoons vinaigrette sauce made with
    lemon juice
    6 drops Pernod

Trim the fennel by cutting off the feathery stalks and the coarse outer leaves and cut across into very thin slices. Pour the dressing over it and mix thoroughly.

PETA'S TUNA FISH SALAD

This is one of the many delicious things we have for lunch when shooting in Spain. We are usually very hungry as breakfast was probably at 7 a.m. and by the time the last drive before lunch has taken place it is 2 p.m. so the sight of the long check cloth covered table is a welcome one. Bottles of red and white wine down the centre and a wonderful assortment of salads and starters. There are no side plates so everything is eaten off a long Spanish bread roll cut in half so all the juice soaks into it – very fattening. To add to the euphoria is the sun and the fantastic backdrop of the Sierra Morena and Segura mountains. The following recipe is both quick and versatile, and can be either a starter or a main course to be eaten in summer in the garden (if there is any sun).

    4 hard–boiled eggs roughly chopped
    1 × 7 oz (200g) tin tuna
    8 oz (225g) onion peeled and chopped,
    (preferably Spanish)
    ½ pint (225g) mayonnaise 2. p.33 or
    Hellman's
    8 oz (225g) cooked potato, cut in chunks
    1 × 12 oz (350g) tin sweetcorn
    1 pinch curry powder
    salt and freshly ground black pepper

Mix all the ingredients together in a big bowl, the mixture should be rather sloppy, so add more than the stated amount of mayonnaise if necessary. Serve as a main course with hot french bread and a green salad. If making it as a starter, omit the potato and the tin of sweetcorn and serve in individual ramekins.

RUSSIAN SALAD

Very quick and easy to make, and if you are really in a hurry use Hellman's mayonnaise and as a last resort tinned petits pois.

    1½ lbs cold cooked potatoes cut into 1″
    (3cm) dice
    8 oz (225g) cold cooked peas
    4 oz (100g) cold cooked carrots cut into ½″
    (2cm) dice
    ½ pint (275ml) mayonnaise 2 p.33
    salt and pepper to taste   **Serves 4–6**

Place all the vegetables in a large bowl and pour the mayonnaise over them whilst they are still slightly warm. Mix well, but be careful not to break up the potatoes. Add more mayonnaise if necessary when the salad is cold so that everything is really well coated. Adjust seasoning if you think it is needed and garnish with a few spring onions.

TOMATO RING

A colourful addition to a buffet and goes well with Chicken Salad *p.85* or Pheasant Cream *p.63*

2 x 14 oz (395g) tins peeled Italian tomatoes
2½ pkts aspic
1 x 4 oz (100g) carton cottage cheese
2 fl oz (660ml) sherry
1 dessertspoon demerara sugar
1 oz (25g) finely chopped spring onion,
shallot or onion
1 teaspoon chopped chives
1 teaspoon chopped parsley
1 teaspoon chopped basil
¼ teaspoon lemon pepper
¼ teaspoon garlic pepper
½ teaspoon salt   **Serves 6−8**

Filling:
1 lb (450g) cold cooked peas
Open the two tins and process for just long enough to break up the tomatoes into a lumpy purée. Bring ½ pint (275ml) of the tomato purée and the sherry up to boiling point and dissolve the aspic in it. Break the cheese up with a fork and add it and all the other ingredients to the rest of the tomato and then pour in the aspic and sherry mixture. Pour into a 1½ pint (850ml) ring mould and allow to set. Turn out just before serving and fill the centre with the cold cooked peas. This also makes a very nice starter in the summer − halve the quantities and pour into individual ramekins. Omit the peas, or use just a few as a garnish.

Puddings

P uddings were not a great item in our household, being generally discouraged on the score of being too fattening, especially as the Head of the Household (sic) always demands cream with everything! However, since the advent of 'Piggy', Lucy's fiancé, things have changed, as he is definately a 'pudding man'. Archie benefits from this spin-off as I have had to resurrect a great many fattening favourites. I had forgotten how delicious so many of these 'nursery' puddings are, but when Piggy is around I have to make plenty as he has been known to have three helpings! Of course, I do think they are a nice ending to a dinner party, though people seem to have less appetite than they used to, and three courses is as much as most people can manage nowadays. Thirty-odd years ago, even when there was still partial rationing, nearly every time you dined out there were four courses. And before the war Archie says he can remember it being perfectly normal to have eight courses.

CHOCCY POTS

Whenever I consult Archie about a menu for a dinner party, or for one of our gourmet shoot lunches and we come to the choice of puddings, I always know what his suggestion will be – 'Choccy Pots' or mousse – no matter how rich the preceding courses. Sometimes he literally feels deprived and chants a sotto voce litany – 'want a choccy pot' until, of course, he gets it. I must say this recipe is simplicity itself, so I ought not to complain.

½ lb (225g) Menier bitter chocolate
2 heaped teaspoons instant coffee dissolved in
1 dessertspoon hot water
1 oz (25g) unsalted butter
4 eggs
1 dessertspoon brandy or liqueur of your choice   **Serves 6**

Break the chocolate into pieces and place in a bowl over hot water together with the instant coffee, brandy or liqueur. When it has melted, break in the egg yolks one by one and stir well. Then add the butter cut into small pieces and stir until melted. The mixture should look shiny. Take the bowl off the hot water and allow to cool. Finally, fold in the stiffly beaten whites of egg and spoon into glasses, or small pots. These freeze very well, so you can always have them as a standby for emergencies as they only take about 1 hour to thaw out.

CRÊME AUX LANGUES DE CHAT

I used to make this with Coffee or Chocolate Langues de Chat biscuits, which seem to be unobtainable nowadays, so you will have to use the plain ones, which are just as good.

This is one of the quickest puddings you can imagine, and provided you have the cream, your unexpected guest will marvel at the speed with which you have produced a dinner party dessert. Virtually all you need is whipped cream, sugar, drinking chocolate and langues de chat biscuits.

1 pint (575ml) double cream	dissolved in a little water
1 tablespoon powdered drinking chocolate	1 teaspoon brandy (optional)
1 dessertspoon caster sugar	1 packet langues de chat biscuits
1 teaspoon Camp coffee or instant coffee	**Serves 6–8**

Whip the cream until it stands up in *soft* peaks, and then fold in the chocolate, sugar, coffee, and brandy. Spoon into a 1½ pint (850ml) soufflé dish. Stick the biscuits vertically all round the outside of the dish and dot the remainder at random in the middle with about 1″ (3cm) sticking out. Put in the fridge to chill. Although a good 'last minute' recipe it is best made a few hours before being eaten as the base of the biscuits then have time to go soft and absorb the flavour.

ELDERBERRY MOUSSE

This is a very unusually flavoured mousse. If you live in the country you are likely to take the profusion of elder bushes all too much for granted, but you shouldn't as they produce the exquisite smelling creamy white flowers which impart a muscatel like flavour to stewed gooseberries. You can make them into a delicate sorbet, (recipe on *p. 98* in this chapter) and an excellent wine *p. 108*. The berries can be made into an original jelly to go with cold meat, you can use them to make an iced soufflé and a fruit mousse. But do not despair if you live in a town. Any time in September that you take a trip to the country, just pick a basketful, take them home, strip the berries off the stalks with a fork and you are ready to roll.

1½ lbs (650g) elderberries	¼ pint (150ml) double cream
4 oz (100g) sugar	½ oz (15g) gelatine
3 eggs	1 tablespoon water
	Serves 6–8

Cook the elderberries over a low heat with 1 tablespoon of the sugar, then place in the liquidizer or Magimix and process until smooth. Rub through a nylon strainer or sieve to remove pips and reheat. Put back in processor and switch on. Take out pusher and break in each egg yolk separately. Then add the sugar and whizz until dissolved. Add the gelatine which you have dissolved in the tablespoon of water, and fold in the cream which has been whipped to soft peaks. Leave to get quite cool, and when the mixture begins to set, fold in the stiffly beaten whites of egg. Cover with cling film and leave to set completely in the fridge.

HONESTY & CHEAT

You may well ask why this pudding is called Honesty & Cheat. I don't know and no one seems to be able to throw any light on it. The recipe was given to me by a cousin who was given it by a friend. Legend has it that the friend, who lived in a castle on the Welsh borders, found it amongst old papers in an attic, written in faded ink on yellowed paper. Though the ingredients are strange, it is a delicious recipe.

8 oz (220g) pinhead oatmeal (obtainable at Health Food Stores)	1 tablespoon cocoa
	1 tablespoon sugar
½ pint (275ml) thick double cream	½ pint (275ml) milk
4 oz (100g) cooking chocolate	1 dessertspoon cornflour
	Serves 4–6

Toast the oatmeal on a baking sheet in the oven until golden brown and crisp. Mix the cornflour in a little of the milk. Heat the chocolate, cocoa and sugar in the remainder and add the cornflour. Bring to the boil and cook for 2–3 minutes, stirring all the time. If it doesn't look thick enough add another teaspoon of cornflour mixed in a little milk. Serve the oatmeal in a dish and the cream and chocolate sauce in two separate jugs. Each guest then helps him/herself to a pile of oatmeal, a puddle of cream and a puddle of chocolate sauce. Very yummy, and a lot more so than the treat we were given once when partridge shooting in Spain.

We were living in an isolated gamekeeper's house, in very primitive conditions −− cooking was done over a log fire. At breakfast we were told that we were to be given something very special. Imagine our horror when the old crone who was the cook bore in plates of breadcrumbs fried in oil and garlic, covered in chocolate sauce!

JEANETTE'S TARTE AUX POMMES

Jeanette was cook to an old friend of mine who lived in a mouldering château in Brittany. Unfortunately Jeanette was often drunk on the local 'alembique' (or Breton calvados), but when sober her apple tart was ambrosial. When I finally winkled the recipe out of her she astonished me by saying that one of the ingredients of her pastry was hard-boiled yolk of egg. It is virtually impossible to roll out because there is no liquid to bind it together so you have to press it into the flan dish with the knuckles of your hand and work it until it covers the dish.

Jeanette's Pastry
    8 oz (225g) plain flour
    3 oz (75g) caster or granulated sugar
    5 oz (150g) unsalted butter
    2 hard−boiled egg yolks, sieved
    pinch salt

Sieve flour and salt into food processor, then add butter cut into small pieces, and the hard−boiled egg yolks. Process until amalgamated and it forms a ball. Butter an 8″ (20cm) flan dish and then sprinkle with flour. Place ball of pastry in the centre and gradually work it towards the sides with the knuckles of your hand. When you have done this put in the fridge for 1 hour. Preheat oven to 375°F 190°C Gas Mark 5, prick the bottom of the pastry, line with foil and fill with dried or ceramic beans and place in the oven for 6 minutes. Remove foil and beans and cook for a further 10−15 minutes. Take out and allow to cool. You can line the flan case with either a confectioner's custard or with a 'marmelade' or thick purée of apple, before finishing off with your topping of overlapping slices of apple.

Filling 1 Confectioner's Custard
    3 oz (75g) sifted plain flour
    2 whole eggs
    4 oz (100g) caster sugar
    1 tablespoon unsalted butter
    ¾ pint (425ml) milk
    1 tablespoon calvados or a few drops of
    vanilla essence

Beat together whole eggs, yolks and sugar in a double boiler over hot water until the mixture falls in a 'ribbon'. Tip in all the flour at one go and beat until smooth then beat in the boiling milk. Put the pan directly on stove over a low heat and whisk until it comes to a boil, then add calvados or vanilla essence and beat again. Pour into a bowl, cover with cling film and allow to cool.

Filling 2 Marmelade de Pommes
    2 lbs peeled, cored & quartered cooking
    apples
    1 oz (25g) butter
    4−6 oz (100−125g) sugar
    1 tablespoon water

Cook apples and butter in a saucepan with a tight fitting lid until soft, then add sugar and continue cooking over a very low heat stirring all the time until it begins to smell of toffee and look golden and caramelized. Allow to cool.

Topping
    2−3 large cooking apples, peeled, cored and
    halved

4 tablespoons redcurrant jelly or apricot jam heated in 1 tablespoon water for glazing
Serves 6−8

Choose filling 1 or 2 and spread evenly over base of flan. Cut apples in very thin slices and lay in concentric overlapping circles on top until you have completely covered the filling layer. Place in a hot oven 400°F 200°C Gas Mark 6 for about 10 minutes or until the apples begin to brown. Be careful the pastry does not burn. Finish by painting on the redcurrant jelly or apricot jam glaze. Serve cold.

LEMON MERINGUE PIE

This is Will Garfit's favourite pudding. We always have to have this and Oxtail Stew when he comes to stay, even in high summer.

Make Shortcrust Pastry as per recipe on *p.39*. Roll out lightly and line an 8″ (20cm) flan dish. Prick bottom and line loosley with foil and beans. Bake 'blind' in a preheated oven at 375°F 190°C Gas Mark 5 for about 10 minutes then lift out the foil and beans. Cook for a further 10 to 15 minutes or until pale gold in colour. Take out and cool.

FILLING
        ½ pint (275ml) milk
        3 egg yolks
        1 oz (25g) cornflour
        3 oz (75g) caster sugar
        grated rind and juice of 1 lemon

Mix the cornflour with a little of the milk. Bring the rest of the milk to the boil and pour onto the cornflour, mix and continue cooking until thick. Add the sugar and stir to dissolve. Beat in the egg yolks one by one and add the grated lemon rind and juice. Pour into the pastry case and cook in a preheated oven at 325°F 160°C Gas Mark 3 for about 15 minutes or until set.

MERINGUE TOPPING
        3 egg whites
        6 oz (175g) granulated sugar   **Serves 4−6**

Beat the egg whites until really stiff, then whisk in 1 dessertspoon of the sugar. Finally fold in the rest of the sugar carefully to keep in as much air as possible. Cover the flan and sprinkle with sugar. Place in a preheated oven at 275°F 140°C Gas Mark 1 for 15−20 minutes until it is golden on top.

GUARDS PUDDING

Definitely a 'Piggy' pudding and always popular with the male guests, but the ladies have also been known to have a surreptitious second helping or a scrape of the dish in the kitchen. Must be served with thick cream, Channel Island if possible. You should use raspberry jam, but strawberry will do and, at a pinch, if the cupboard is bare try plum or apricot.

        3 oz (75g) unsalt butter
        3 oz (75g) caster or granulated sugar
        3 oz (75g) cake crumbs – I use trifle sponges
        process in the Magimix
        2 eggs
        3 tablespoons raspberry (or other) jam
        ½ teaspoon bicarbonate of soda
        Serves 4–6

Process or beat the butter and sugar until light and fluffy, then break in the eggs one by one and process for 15 seconds. Add cake crumbs and process for a few seconds or until mixed and then add bicarbonate of soda which has been dissolved in a little boiling water. Turn into a greased pudding basin, cover with greased foil and steam for 2 hours, then turn out.

LEMON STONE CREAM

This is a very old Victorian recipe, and the original stated that you should climb a pair of kitchen steps and pour the cream from a height. I always imagine the little kitchen maid in her long skirts being made to scramble up the steps and pour the cream into one of those old fashioned mixing bowls, white inside and yellow outside, and woe betide her if she spilt the cream onto the flagstone floor.

1 pint (575ml) double cream
2 lemons
2 tablespoons sugar
grated rind of 1 lemon   **Serves 6−8**

Squeeze the juice of the lemons into a fair sized bowl. Spread some newspaper on the kitchen floor and stand the bowl on it. Bring the cream to the boil over a low heat, and as it is just beginning to come up the sides of the pan, start pouring it in a thin stream onto the lemon juice from as great a height as you can manage. Now stir in the sugar and the grated peel and pour into glasses or small pots. Cool and place in the fridge. Best made the day before eating. If possible use cream which has been in your fridge for a day or two, preferably just before it goes out of date. For some reason it sets better. Freezes well.

MERINGUE CAKE

This is a rather theatrical pudding which looks nice if you are having a buffet supper. The great joy is that you can make the meringue rounds beforehand and store them in a tin or in the deep freeze.

4 egg whites
8 oz (200g) caster sugar
½ pint (175ml) double cream
½ pint (175ml) single cream
1 dessertspoon drinking chocolate
1 teaspoon orange juice
1 teaspoon grated orange peel **Serves 8–10**
To decorate: crystalized cherries, violets and
angelica, and walnut halves.

Whip the egg whites very stiffly, then beat in the sugar in 4 lots and continue beating until thick and creamy. Now place 3 8″ (20cm) cake tins upside down and cover with foil, shiny side up, Dip a piece of kitchen paper in oil and smear it all over the foil. Now divide the meringue mixture into 3 parts and spready evenly over each tin. Place in the oven and switch on to 300°F 150°C Gas Mark 2, leave for half-an-hour, then turn down to 250°F 140°C Gas Mark 1 for 2 hours. Test with a skewer and if it comes out clean they are done. If it comes out sticky, try very carefully to remove the meringue from the foil and turn each one over. Leave for a further hour or until completely dry and your skewer comes out clean, then remove and allow to cool. If your party is not for several days, store in an airtight tin or in the freezer. The morning or afternoon before your dinner party, whip the two creams together until they are fairly stiff, but not buttery, and divide into two. Into the first lot stir a dessertspoon of caster sugar, the orange juice and the chocolate powder. Spread this mixture on two of the meringue rounds and place one on top of the other, finishing off with the third one. Stir a dessertspoon of caster sugar into the second lot of cream and if you feel inclined, a teaspoon of brandy or orange curaçao, then spread all over the 'cake' on top and round the sides, smoothing with a palette knife until it looks just like an iced cake. Decorate according to your fancy with cherries, violets, angelica and halved walnuts or whatever you feel like. You can do all sorts of things to vary it – use more chocolate and decorate with grated chocolate, flavour wth coffee, just use whipped cream and sugar and sprinkle fresh raspberries or strawberries between each layer, in which case it becomes a 'Vacherin'. Also delicious as a birthday cake.

MRS FORD'S PUDDING

This was one of the 'pièces de résistance' produced by the daleswoman who cooked for us when we were shooting grouse in Yorkshire. It is very rich, so a little goes a long way.

Crust
8 oz (225g) digestive biscuits
3 oz (75g) melted butter

Melt the butter and crush the biscuits. Mix together and put half the mixture in the bottom of a soufflé dish.

Filling
4 oz (100g) unsalt butter
8 oz (225g) sugar
2 well beaten eggs
½ teacup chopped nuts
2 teacups well drained, crushed pineapple,
or better still fresh pineapple chopped
coarsely in the Magimix or liquidizer.
6 fl oz (185ml) double cream, whipped in
soft peaks **Serves 6–8**

Cream butter and sugar, add beaten eggs and whisk well. Cover crust in dish. Add a thin layer of pineapple, a layer of chopped nuts and then another layer of pineapple. Spread on the whipped cream and top with the remaining crust. Serve very cold. Freezes well.

QUEEN'S PUDDING

Another old fashioned nursery pudding which always goes down well.

4 oz (100g) fresh breadcrumbs
½ pint (275ml) milk
3 eggs
½ oz (15g) butter
2 tablespoons sugar for the custard
4 oz (100g) sugar for the meringue topping
½ lb (200g) raspberry, strawberry or plum
jam   **Serves 4—6**

Bring the milk, sugar and butter to the boil, then pour over the breadcrumbs. Add the egg yolks and stir well. Bake in a moderate oven 325°F 160°C Gas Mark 2 until set. Remove from oven and spread with jam. Whip the egg whites until very stiff and beat in 2 oz (50g) of the sugar, then fold in all but 1 tablespoon. Spoon on top of the pudding and sprinkle with the remaining tablespoon of sugar. Bake in preheated oven at 350°F 175°C Gas Mark 4 until pale golden in colour – about 10 to 15 minutes.

TREACLE TART

I apologise for giving such an everyday recipe, but I find people have got so used to buying the ready-made ones that they have forgotten what the real thing tastes like – so, I don't apologise after all!

6 oz (175g) plain flour
4 oz (100g) cooking butter
1—2 tablespoons cold water
pinch salt
2 oz (50g) white breadcrumbs
6 tablespoons golden syrup
1 egg beaten with 1 tablespoon water
                                       Serves 4—6

Sieve flour and salt into Magimix or processor and drop in butter cut into small pieces. Process for 15 seconds and then add water, process again until mixture forms a ball. Take out and cover in cling film and put to rest in refrigerator for 1 hour. Butter an 8″ (20cm) flan dish and cover with ⅔ of the thinly rolled out pastry. Spread the breadcrumbs evenly over the bottom and then spoon over the golden syrup. Make a lattice pattern over the top with the remaining ⅓ pastry and brush with egg and water. Place on the middle shelf of preheated oven at 400°F 200°C Gas Mark 6 for 12 minutes then reduce to 350°F 175°C Gas Mark 4 for 20—25 minutes.

COUSIN CONSTANCE'S TRIFLE

When Cousin Constance produced this trifle I utterly refused to believe that she had made it with custard powder. Knowing how meticulous she is, I had visions of her slaving over a hot stove making some special kind of egg custard in a 'bain marie' – but not a bit of it, the secret she said lay in beating the custard mixture really well so that it wasn't stodgy. Anyway I highly recommend it as being both delicious to eat and quick to make.

8 trifle sponges
strawberry or raspberry jam
4 fl oz (100ml) sherry
½ pint (275ml) milk
1 tablespoon custard powder
1 tablespoon caster sugar

To decorate:
¼ pint (150ml) cream whipped, glacé
cherries, angelica   **Serves 6–8**

Cut the sponges in half and spread liberally with jam and then place them in the bottom of a bowl, preferably glass. Fill in the gaps with more jam and pour on the sherry. Place a plate on top and then a 2 lb (900g) weight and leave overnight in the fridge. Make a smooth paste of the custard powder with a little of the cold milk and bring the rest to the boil then pour it onto the custard mixture. Tip it all back into the saucepan and let it cook for 2 to 3 minutes, stirring constantly, then put into a bowl and cover tightly with cling film to prevent a skin forming. Allow to cool then put in the fridge. The following morning take out, remove the cling film and beat really well until it is light and creamy. Remove the plate and weight from the sponge and jam and pour the custard over it, put back in the fridge and leave to set before decorating with the whipped cream, cherries and angelica.

ICED STRAWBERRY SOUFFLÉ

This is the one ice cream that cannot fail, does not go splintery and needs no stirring. You can also use any fruit, but blackberries, elderberries and quinces should be cooked in a minimum amount of water before puréeing. Fruit containing a lot of pips should be sieved after you have processed it.

8 oz (225g) fresh or frozen strawberries
½ pint (275ml) double cream
¼ pint (150ml) single cream
3 egg whites
6 oz (175g) caster sugar
1 tablespoon lemon juice   **Serves 8—10**

Purée the strawberries with the lemon juice. Whip the two creams together into soft peaks and fold into the fruit purée. Whip the egg whites until they are *really* stiff and add the sugar, a tablespoon at a time and continue to whip until the mixture is *really* thick. Fold into the fruit and cream, spoon into a soufflé dish and freeze. Take out of the freezer 1 hour before you are going to eat. On occasions I have left it too late, the result being that my guests needed an ice pick and not a spoon!

BROWN BREAD ICE CREAM

This is a very old Victorian recipe. If you feel too idle to make the vanilla ice yourself, you can use a block of really good quality bought ice cream, allow it to get soft enough to manipulate, and then fold in the toasted breadcrumbs.

Vanilla Ice Cream

4 egg yolks
1 pint (575ml) single cream
3 oz (75g) caster sugar
1 vanilla pod   **Serves 6—8**

Beat the egg yolks with the sugar in a bowl over hot water until light and fluffy. Bring cream to the boil with the vanilla pod, which you then remove. Pour the cream onto the egg yolks and stir over the hot water until it thickens. Pour into a container and place a layer of cling film over the mixture to prevent it forming a skin whilst it cools. When cold put into the freezer. Scrape the sides down every half—an—hour until nearly set, then fold in the breadcrumbs. Serve with any kind of sharp fruit purée such as plum, damson or raspberry.

For the crumbs

½ stale Granary loaf
caster sugar

Cut crust off the loaf and process the bread into fairly coarse crumbs in the Magimix or liquidizer. Spread on a baking tray and sprinkle with caster sugar. Place in a moderate oven 300°F 150°C Gas Mark 2 until brown (but not burnt).

BLACKCURRANT LEAF OR ELDERFLOWER SORBET

A very refreshing, 'tangy' sorbet to help the digestion after a heavy main course. The blackcurrant leaves are best picked in early summer, when they are young. This is basically a lemon sorbet recipe which you can use on its own, or as a change use an infusion of elderflowers to flavour it.

1 handful – about 2 oz (50g) of young
blackcurrant leaves
or
1 tablespoon dried elderflowers or 2 fresh
heads of elderflower
½ pint (275ml) lemon juice
1 pint (575ml) water
8 oz (225g) lump sugar
2 stiffly beaten whites egg   **Serves 4–6**

Before you start, place a metal bowl in the freezer, I use a Le Creuset casserole or an anodized metal loaf tin, this makes the freezing process much quicker. Bring water and sugar slowly to the boil, stirring until sugar is dissolved. Boil furiously for 5 minutes and then pour onto the blackcurrant leaves. Cover and leave to get cool, then strain and add to the lemon juice. Pour the liquid into your chosen container and stir every half-an-hour until it thickens to the consistency of very thick mayonnaise. Now add the stiffly beaten whites of egg and stir well. Leave for 10 to 15 minutes and then beat furiously with hand or electric beaters. This will make it fluffy and not splintery. Take out just before you eat the first course. Scoop out and serve in individual glasses with a sprig of blackcurrant leaf on each.

TANGERINE SORBET

This is an eye–catching pudding to serve after a rather rich meal and isn't nearly as difficult to make as you might think. Try if possible to get real tangerines, as the flavour is better and it is easier to winkle out the insides.

12 tangerines (or similar) plus a few extra in
case they are not juicy enough
juice of 2 lemons
8 oz (225g) lump sugar
½ pint (275ml) fruit juice (tangerine &
lemon mixed)
1 pint (575ml) water
12 bay or laurel leaves
2 whites of egg stiffly whipped   **Serves 12**

Cut 2″ (4½cm) rounds from the top of each tangerine and ease out the flesh with a teaspoon. Put the empty tangerine cases and 'hats' in the freezer on a baking tray. Process the flesh in the blender or Magimix for a few seconds and then press as much of the juice as possible through a plastic or stainless steel strainer or a sieve. Add the lemon juice and if you don't have your ½ pint (275ml) of liquid make up the quantity with more tangerine juice. Bring the water and sugar slowly to the boil, stirring to dissolve the sugar and boil fast for 5 minutes. Allow to cool and then add to the fruit juice. Pour into a bowl and put in the fast freezing part of your freezer. Follow the recipe on *p.98* for Blackcurrant Leaf Sorbet. When you have beaten in the stiffly whipped egg whites, fill the tangerine cases with the mixture. Place a 'hat' on each and a bayleaf and replace in the freeze until needed. Take out of the freezer while you are eating your first course. Serve on a large dish arranged in a pyramid, or pile them up in a bowl.

Supper Dishes

My definition of a supper dish is something which you produce when you are just 'family'. Generally something which wouldn't be considered grand enough for a dinner party.

For me there is often a last minute panic when I come in from pigeon shooting, fishing or gardening and haven't until that minute thought of what I am going to cook for supper.

Only cheese in the fridge means a Cheese Soufflé p. 99 – Archie's very hungry, Corned Beed hash p. 100 – Archie wants to cook, Coats Curry p. 101 and so on. It just all depends on what you feel like, what's available, the time factor, and what's good on the telly, as we almost always eat on our laps 'en famille'.

CHEESE SOUFFLÉ

Until fairly recently I took fright at the thought of making a soufflé and when Archie asked for a cheese one I always used to change the conversation. But one day I thought I'd have a go and, in fact, it really isn't at all difficult. This is a basic recipe, but you can vary it by using other ingredients such as spinach or fish.

2 oz (50g) butter
2 oz (50g) flour
1 oz (25g) very finely chopped shallot
¼ pint (150ml) milk
5 egg yolks
6 – 7 egg whites
4 oz (100g) grated parmesan
2 oz (100g) grated emmental

or
6 oz (175g) strong cheddar if
these are not available
1 teaspoon made mustard
1 teaspoon Worcester Sauce
salt and pepper   **Serves 4 – 6**

Melt the butter in a large saucepan and cook the chopped shallot for a few minutes, then add the flour and cook for 2 minutes. Add the milk and beat with a wire balloon whisk over a low heat until the mixture thickens. Pull off the stove and add the egg yolks one at a time and the grated cheese in dribs and drabs until it is all mixed in. Cook for a few minutes until the cheese has begun to melt and add the mustard, Worcester Sauce, and plenty of salt and pepper. Cool a little, then fold in the stiffly beaten egg whites and spoon into a buttered soufflé dish. It is better not to fold in the egg whites too vigorously – even if you leave a few blobs it doesn't matter. The great thing is not to let the air escape. Cook in a preheated oven at 350°F 175°C Gas Mark 4 for 35 to 40 minutes until well risen and golden brown on top. Serve immediately or it will collapse.

CORNED BEEF HASH

One of Archie's favourite supper dishes when we are on our own and I don't know what else to give him.

1 × 12oz (350g) tin corned beef cut in dice
8 oz (225g) peeled and diced potato
8 oz (225g) peeled and roughly chopped
onion
1 tablespoon sunflower oil
1 dash Worcester Sauce
salt and pepper (or Archie's condiment)
p.18

Serves 2

Heat the oil in a thick frying pan and add the potato and onion, cover with a lid and cook over a low heat until soft. Now add the corned beef and the seasonings and cook over a moderate heat uncovered until a thick brown crust has formed on the bottom. In America it is served with a fried egg on top – Archie only gets that as a great treat, but it is quite delicious as the egg goes very well, and it does make a more substantial dish.

MOUSSAKA

This is a very filling luncheon or supper dish. The first time I ever had it was in a now sadly defunct Greek restaurant in Kensington. It was cooked in the traditional way with fried aubergines, but although I have made it like this I think it can be a bit rich and oily, so I just use the raw sliced aubergines as they are – they cook perfectly well between the layers of mince and provided you butter or oil the dish they won't stick. I give the traditional recipe, but you can take your choice.

1 lb (450g) mince – preferably lamb if you
can get it.
1½ lbs (675g) aubergines
8 oz (225g) peeled and chopped onion
2 cloves garlic finely chopped
3 tablespoons concentrated tomato purée
¼ pint (150ml) water and 1 beef stock cube,
or stock
¼ pint (150ml) oil for frying
½ teaspoon coriander seeds
1 dessertspoon basil
salt and plenty of ground black pepper
Topping
½ pint (275ml) single cream
2 egg yolks
1 dessertspoon parmesan cheese **Serves 4–6**
or

Slice the aubergines in rounds but do not peel. Spread out on a dish and sprinkle with salt and leave for 1 hour. Place in a colander and rinse in cold water, drain and pat dry with kitchen paper. Heat the oil in a frying pan until smoking hot and fry the aubergine rounds until golden then lift out and drain on kitchen paper. Brown the onions and mince in the remaining oil and then add the stock, tomato purée, basil, coriander, salt and pepper. Line a casserole with aubergine slices and then add alternate layers of mince and aubergine until you have used it all up. Cover and place in a preheated oven at 300°F 150°C Gas Mark 2 for 2 hours. Turn the oven up to 350°F 175°C Gas Mark 4, take the lid off the casserole and pour over the cream in which you have beaten up the egg yolks and parmesan. Cook the moussaka for a further 20–25 minutes or until the creamy custard is brown on top and set.

COAT'S CURRY

When Archie was in The Hague before the war he and his father used to go to the Hotel des Indes where the speciality was a 'Ryztavel' – quite literally a rice table or Indonesian curry smorgasbord. A Dutch friend of mine says the usual number of dishes is twelve though in Java it can go up to one hundred and twenty. To be authentic each course is meant to be borne in by a beautiful maiden. History doesn't relate if they were in Archies's case, and he isn't telling. This particular kind of curry is sweet and is Archie's speciality, and I have no hesitation in saying that he makes a far better one than I do. The great secret is long slow cooking, and as with casseroles it is even better when reheated. You can use any ingredient such as chicken or beef but I usually use pigeon breasts.

8 oz (225g) pigeon breasts cut into ½″ (1cm)
dice
4 oz (100g) diced apple
4 oz (100g) chopped onion
2 oz (50g) any kind dried fruit
1 dessertspoon bramble jelly

1 dessertspoon mango chutney
1 teaspoon black treacle
1 teaspoon mixed herbs
2 cloves garlic
2 teaspoons hot curry paste
2 teaspoons mild curry powder
½ teaspoon salt
oil for frying

Heat about 1 tablespoon oil in a thick frying pan, or better still the oil from the curry paste pot. Fry the apple and onion for a few minutes, then add the diced pigeon breasts and all the other ingredients. Cook on a very low heat for about 1 hour, stirring every so often to prevent sticking. Cover and continue cooking for a further hour. At the end of this time the curry should look nearly black and very thick. Serve with rice and poppadums, sliced bananas, sliced tomato and onion, and coconut if you like it.

LASAGNE

A marvellous freezer standby, as if you make it in a shallow foil dish you can whip it straight out of your deep freeze and into the oven. Even without a microwave you should have the perfect supper in less than an hour.

Lasagne

    12 squares Barilla lasagne (plain or green)
    1 quart (1 litre) boiling salted water
    1 tablespoon olive oil

The Barilla lasagne made with eggs says on the packet that it is precooked and that you don't need to boil it, but I have never dared to do this in case I ended up with several layers of india—rubber. So I throw the squares of pasta into fiercely boiling water and cook for about 5 minutes. It is very important to have a really large container for this, so I use a preserving pan. When cooked, drain and lay the lasagne out on one or two clean tea towels whilst you are making the two sauces.

Meat Sauce

    8—12 oz (225g—350g) fresh mince or
    minced cooked meat
    2 cloves garlic finely chopped
    2 medium or 1 large onion finely chopped
    1 level teaspoon Italian mixed herbs and at
    least 2 bayleaves
    1 teaspoon crumbled basil (frozen or dried)
    1 small tin concentrated tomato purée
    1 small tin tomatoes
    1—2 tablespoons olive oil
    salt and pepper   **Serves 6—8**

Heat oil in pan until smoking, throw in onion and garlic and turn down heat. Stir and cook until golden brown. Now add meat and cook for a few minutes. Lastly put in all the other ingredients and stir well. Cover and cook over a low heat until tender and sauce has reduced. Set aside.

Cheese sauce

    4 oz (100g) butter
    4 oz (100g) flour
    2 pints (1 litre) milk
    8 oz (225g) grated fresh parmesan cheese,
    (Don't use the tubs of ready
    grated parmesan, it tasts of sawdust.) Failing
    fresh parmesan use strong
    cheddar.

Melt butter in a large saucepan, an 8 pint (3 litre) one, if possible. Tip in the flour and cook for a few minutes, stirring all the time. Pull the saucepan off the stove and pour in the milk slowly, whisking constantly with a large balloon whisk. When it is all incorporated, return to the stove and stir with a wooden spoon until the sauce thickens. Cook for a few minutes over a low heat stirring continually. Add the cheese and go on cooking until the cheese has melted.

    If not freezing the lasagne, I use a square, shallow earthenware dish. An oval one will do but the squares of pasta will be more difficult to arrange. It is most important to layer the lasagne so that the squares overlap and thus keep the meat and cheese sauce separate. Start with a good layer of meat sauce at the bottom. Now lay 4 of the sheets carefully on top. You may have trim them. Be sure that the outside edges project slightly up the sides of the dish. Now spread a layer of cheese sauce, then another layer of pasta and so on, ending up with a layer of cheese sauce on top. You should have 2 layers of meat and 2 layers of cheese sauce. Sprinkle a light covering of grated cheese over the top and cook in a preheated oven 325°F 160°C Gas Mark 3 for ¾ of an hour or until it is brown and bubbling.

SANTÉ'S TAGLIATELLE

This heavenly pasta dish of Mr Santé is hard to resist, but if you choose the Calves Liver with Sage *p.80* as a main course, it is almost impossible to do it justice as Mr Santé's idea of a small helping is enough for a very hungry prize fighter. It is an excellent 'quickie' as all the ingredients except the cheese can be kept in your store cupboard or freezer.

1 packet Barilla tagliatelle, either plain or green
1 tablespoon olive oil
2 oz (50g) butter
1 medium onion, coarsely chopped
1 large clove garlic
1 small tin peeled Italian tomatoes
6 oz (50g) finely diced ham or rashers of bacon
2 tins button mushrooms

2 teaspoons basil
or
1 teaspoon Italian mixed herbs
1 large clove garlic
1 carton double cream or ten pieces frozen cream
4 oz (100g) grated parmesan or cheddar cheese
salt and freshly ground black pepper

Serves 6–8

Heat butter in a saucepan and cook the onions and garlic until golden, add all the rest of the ingredients except the cream, pasta and olive oil and cook for about 10 minutes. Meanwhile, bring 2 quarts (2 litres) water to the boil, add salt and the olive oil. Throw in the tagliatelle and cook for about 10 minutes or until 'al dente'. Drain the pasta and tip into a large bowl or dish, add cream to the sauce and pour over the pasta, turn and mix it well, sprinkle cheese on top. Accompany by a crisp salad of radiccio, chicory, watercress or curly endive and hot crusty french bread, which is a must to mop up the sauce.

SPANISH OMELETTE

This is staple fare in Spain when we go and shoot partridges with Lucy's godfather. Along with all the other outdoor shooting lunch fare it always figures among the starters, where it is served cold, cut in wedges.

6 eggs beaten roughly
4 oz (100g) peeled chopped onion
4 oz (100g) roughly cut up cooked potato
oil for frying
salt and pepper

Serves 4

Put about 1 dessertspoon oil in an 8″ (20cm) thick cast iron frying pan and heat. Brown the onion in this then add the potato, cook for a few minutes and then add to the bowl in which you have beaten the eggs. Wipe the pan clean with kitchen paper, put in a little oil and let it get really hot, then pour in the egg, onion and potatoes. Stir with a fork occasionally for the first couple of minutes, then turn down the heat and let the omelette cook slowly. When the bottom half looks firm put a spatula or egg lifter underneath and slide onto a plate. Now invert the frying pan over the top and turn over, replace on stove and cook until set. If you don't feel you can manage this just put it under the grill for a minute or two to set – it should be quite firm but not dry. Eat hot or cold cut in wedges.

SHOOTER'S LUNCHES

These are the very bane of my existence as I have to produce a packed lunch for Archie nearly every day when he goes out pigeon shooting. The following are a few random ideas which are suitable for those who want a pocketable meal to go fishing or shooting. When producing a portable lunch for 8 or so hungry shooters and beaters I find it is much easier to produce individual packs than to dish things out, as this then leaves you freer to dole out drinks and soup.

ARCHIE'S FAVOURITE SANDWICH

Archie never tires of telling me that there was hell to pay if his father didn't get this every time he went out shooting. The trouble is that the oatcakes tends to fall out of the bap, so I usually whizz all the ingredients up with a little softened butter in the Magimix which makes it stick together better.

2 baps
6 rashers fat streaky bacon
1 triangular or 2 round oatcakes
1 oz (25g) softened butter
salt and pepper

Heat the baps in the oven until they are *just* crisp on the outside. Cut a small round in the top with the kitchen scissors and pull out the soft middle so you have a hollow shell. Fry the bacon until crisp and then crumble the oatcake into the bacon fat. Fry for a few seconds but do not let it burn. Place the bacon, oatcake, butter and bacon fat in the Magimix and whizz for a couple of seconds. Stuff tightly into the two baps and stick the tops back on. The bacon and oatcake mixture goes well with a fried egg for breakfast, and if you want a luxury sandwich you can put a fried egg on top.

BACON & PEANUT BUTTER SANDWICH

This is the great Peanut Butter Conversion Kit. Many of our guests when I have politely enquired if they like Peanut Butter have expressed an aversion and said they would prefer not to have it as part of their packed lunch. but even some of the most hardened cases have been reformed by this treatment. Another of Archie's specials. He met it in America where he says you can buy it at any drugstore.

4 rounds of bread spread thickly with peanut
butter
4 rashers crisply fried bacon
plenty of salt and pepper

Crumble or snip the bacon over the peanut butter rounds, season well and clap together.

TWO TIER EGG & TOMATO BAP

1 salad bap
1 tomato thinly sliced
1 dessertspoon Rondelé or Tartare cheese
1 heaped teaspoon sugar
Archie's Condiment *p.18*
1 hard—boiled egg
1 dessertspoon Hellman's Mayonnaise
1 spring onion sliced in thin rounds
1 heaped teaspoon finely chopped parsley
salt and ground black pepper

Slice the bap across twice but do not sever the slices. Heat in the oven until just crisp. Butter. In the top section spread the cheese, then lay the sliced tomato on top, sprinkle on the sugar and plenty of pepper mix. Squash up the egg and mix with the mayonnaise, spring onion, parsley and plenty of salt and pepper and stuff into the bottom half. You can vary this by putting prawns into the mayonnaise instead of the hard—boiled egg.

Preserves

H ome-made jams and jellies are a must if you live in the country and you can experiment with all kinds of hedgerow fruits such as wild plums, if you happen to come across any, sloes and of course elderberries, blackberries and wild crab apples. The basic recipe for jelly is the same so I have just given those which are my favourites. Elderberries and blackberries will need some apple with them to provide the pectin to make them set. The other preserve which gets devoured in great quantities in this house is marmalade, for which I give my two favourite recipes.

SEVILLE MARMALADE

2 lbs (900g) Seville Oranges
4 pints (2 litres) water
4 lbs demerara sugar
juice of 1 lemon

Squeeze oranges and tie pips up separately in a piece of muslin. Cut up the peel as thick or thin as you wish, or do what I do and stick it in the Magimix to save time and effort. Put into a preserving pan with the pips, water, orange and lemon juice and bring slowly to the boil uncovered. Cook until the peel is soft and the liquid has reduced by half. Now stir in the sugar until it has dissolved (it helps to warm it up beforehand in the oven). Bring back to the boil, put in a walnut–sized piece of butter and keep skimming. Put a plate in the fridge and when you think setting point has been reached, drop a little marmalade on the plate. If it wrinkles when you run a finger over it the marmalade has set. If not, keep on boiling until it does. Wash and dry some jars and heat in the oven. Take out and fill with marmalade right up to the top then cover tightly with squares of cling film. When the jars are cold there should be a small hollow depression in the top of each. This shows that a vacuum has formed and your preserve is airtight and therefore no moulds can enter.

THICK DARK MARMALADE

This is quite my favourite, but some people don't like it as it has a rather strong orangey flavour.

3 lbs (1.4kg) Seville oranges
6 pints (3 litres) water

6 lb (2.8kg) Dark Muscovado sugar
juice of 2 lemons

Follow the above recipe but boil the fruit for at least 2 hours or until it has reduced by more than half before adding the sugar. Pot and cover as above.

APPLE JELLY

4 lbs (1.8kg) crab, cooking or windfall apples

2 pints (1 litre) water
sugar

Wash apples, cut out any bad bits and cut up roughly. Put into a pan with the water and cook until mushy. Strain, then put back into pan with 1¼ lbs (550g) sugar to each pint liquid. Proceed as above.

SOPHIE'S CHUTNEY

This is one of the best chutneys you will ever eat. It came via Cousin Constance from a cook who had been in service with her husband's family. I suffer with this in the same way as the Oxtail Stew, Archie never thinks it is as good as hers. Every year I keep on trying for a 'Gold' but only ever get a 'Bronze' or 'Silver'!

You can make chutney of almost anything provided you use fruit, dried fruit, sugar, vinegar and spices and cook the mixture until it looks really thick. A good guideline is 4 lbs (1.8kg) fruit and vegetable (including onion or shallot), 8 oz (225g) dried fruit, 1½ pints (850ml) vinegar, and spices of your choice. It is fun to experiment but I always come back to the one below.

3 lbs (1.4kg) onions	2 pints (1 litre) malt vinegar
3 lbs (1.4kg) green tomatoes	1 ½ lbs (675g) demerara sugar
4 lbs (1.8kg) apples	1 teaspoon salt
1 lb (450g) sultanas	½ dessertspoon allspice
1 lb (450g) preserved stem ginger without	½ dessertspoon peppercorns
the syrup	½ dessertspoon dried red chillies
6 pieces root ginger crushed	A further 1 lb (450g) sugar

Chop fruit, sultanas and stem ginger either by hand or in the Magimix. Add everything except the last 1 lb (450g) sugar. The recipe says tie up the spices in a bag but I think it is nicer not to do this as the flavours permeate better. Boil gently for 4 hours, add the last lot of sugar and boil for another 3 hours or until it looks almost black and is very thick. Heat the jars and fill with the chutney, then cover with cling film. This is best if kept for a few months before using and is really improved the longer you keep it.

REDCURRANT JELLY

3 lbs (1.4kg) redcurrants
¾ pint (425ml) water
sugar

Wash fruit and put into a preserving pan with the water. Simmer over a low heat until the fruit is cooked and pulpy. Strain through a jelly bag or tea towel, measure the liquid and put into a pan. Add 1 lb (450g) sugar to each pint (575ml) liquid. Stir until dissolved then bring slowly to the boil. Boil rapidly until setting point is reached (probably about 10 minutes) then put into small pots.

GOOSEBERRY & MINT JELLY

4 lbs (1.8kg) unripe gooseberries	1 good bunch mint plus
water	3 tablespoons finely chopped mint
sugar	2 drops green colouring (optional)

Wash gooseberries and cook in just enough water to cover with the bunch of mint until tender and pulpy. Strain and cook with 1 lb (450g) sugar to each pint (575ml) juice until set. Add chopped mint and stir well. Add green colouring if you wish.

GOOSEBERRY & ELDERFLOWER JELLY

This is a delicate and deliciously fragrant jelly with a taste of muscatel grapes. Just follow the above recipe but instead of cooking the gooseberries with a bunch of mint use 6−8 heads of elderflower.

APPLE & ELDERBERRY

3 lbs (1.4kg) elderberries	water
3 lbs (1.4kg) apples	sugar

Wash and cut up the apples and cook in just enough water to cover until tender. Follow the same procedure for the elderberries. Strain through a jelly bag and add ¾ lb (350g) sugar to each pint (575ml) of the mixed juices. Continue as before.

ROWAN & APPLE JELLY

Rowanberries are very bitter if used on their own to make a jelly, so it is best to mix them with apple. This is delicious with rich game dishes and for use in cooking, the slightly bitter−sweet and tangy taste is a good foil for mallard and grouse or venison.

1½ lbs (675g) ripe rowanberries	sugar
1½ lbs (675g) cooking apples or crab apples	juice of 1 lemon
water	

Cook the rowanberries and wash and cut up apples in just enough water to cover until they are mushy. Strain through a jelly bag into a pan and add 1 lb (450g) sugar to each pint (575ml) juice. Add the lemon juice and bring to the boil, stirring until the sugar has dissolved. Boil fast until setting point has been reached. Put in the usual way into small pots.

QUINCE JELLY

4 lbs (1.8kg) quinces	sugar
water	juice of 2 lemons

Wash and cut up the quinces finely or process in the Magimix, put in a pan and cover with water. Cook until really soft then strain. Add 1 lb (450g) sugar to each pint (575ml) of juice. Put into a pan with the lemon juice and boil until set as above.

You can make a Quince Cheese with the strained pulp. Push as much pulp through a sieve as possible and to each 1 lb (450g) add 1 lb (450g) sugar. Put in a pan over a very low heat and stir constantly until it becomes really thick and dark. Line a shallow tray with foil and pour in the mixture. When cold wrap in more foil and store, it will keep perfectly all right in an airtight tin, but once you open it put it in the fridge. For a change use as an accompaniment to cheese and cold meats. This is what the Spanish call 'Membrillo'.

WINES & LIQUEURS

I have only ever been successful with one kind of wine, namely Elderflower. When it works this is like a delicate dessert wine made from muscatel grapes. My best effort was to produce it in a decanter some years ago for our late friend Ralph Cobbold who was then Managing Director of Justerini & Brooks. He savoured and snuffled it in the appropriate manner and said he thought it was a very drinkable Frontignan dessert wine. However he soon twigged that all was not what it seemed as we couldn't keep straight faces, but luckily he took it all in good part. So much so that he took a bottle up to try out in the Directors' lunch room. They were taken in, but did not see the joke and were most stuffy about the whole thing.

ELDERFLOWER WINE

1 pint (575ml) creamy white elderflowers	3 lbs (1.4kg) sugar
2 lemons	1 gallon (4 litres) boiling water
2 rounded teaspoons Boots Wine Yeast Compound	

Prepare the yeast compound 6 hours before you start. Mix 2 rounded teaspoons of the compound in ¼ pint (150ml) tepid water and pour into a small bottle, (I use a small empty tonic water bottle). Screw cap on tightly and shake well, then loosen the cap and leave at room temperature for 6 hours. Pick the elderflowers on a dry sunny day. Snip the florets off the stalks with a pair of scissors and press them into a pint mug then put in a large china bowl or well washed and sterilized plastic pail. Peel the lemons thinly (without any white pith adhering) and add to the flowers together with the sugar. Pour on the boiling water and stir until the sugar has dissolved then add the juice of the 2 lemons. Leave until it has reached blood heat, or when it feels tepid on the back of the hand, then add the yeast compound to the tepid elderflower mixture or 'must'. Cover container with a clean tea towel and leave for 3 days stirring twice daily.

Sterilize a gallon glass jar (from Boots), strain the wine and pour into the jar. Insert a fermentation lock (also obtainable from Boots) which you have half filled with water. Leave the wine to ferment at room temperature until the air lock has stopped making rude noises – about 6 weeks. Take out the air lock and siphon off the wine through a piece of plastic tubing. This is best described in the following way. Place the glass jar on a table, insert the tubing so that an end hangs down lower than the level of the bottom of the jar. Contort yourself so that you can take a suck at the tube and with any luck the wine will then dribble into a well sterilized bucket or bowl on the floor. When you have extracted all except the sediment wash out the jar and pour back the wine. Cork tightly and place in a cool dark place until it is crystal clear, at the end of which time put it into clean sterilized wine bottles. Keep for a year, or for as long as your willpower will allow!

If you are making more than one gallon it is worth buying a filter kit and fining crystals, but it really isn't necessary, and in the old days I used to make it with ordinary Baker's Yeast and it seemed just as good. All the technology can be bought at Boots but I don't understand the intricacies of specific gravity so it is really up to you if you want to do it the hard way – the old cottager's ways seems to work just as well.

LEMON VODKA

A very potent drink so you only need a liqueur glassful to go with your smoked salmon, Smoked Trout Pâté *p.55* or Gravadlax *p.44*. It is very easy to make.

> 1 bottle vodka
> 1 large lemon

Peel the rind of the lemon very thinly with none of the white pith adhering. Try and keep it in one piece if possible as it looks nicer. Pour a little vodka out of the bottle – this will avoid the Archimedes Syndrome. Push the long twist of lemon peel into the bottle, fill with a little more vodka if necessary and screw on the cap. Place in the deep freeze. Ready for use after 24 hours but the longer you keep it there the better it is. Use straight out of the freezer.

SLOE GIN

This recipe also applies to wild plums if (as we are), you are lucky enough to be able to find them. Forty—odd years ago Lord Rank planted them as partridge belts on his shoot. They are now luxuriant and produce a profusion of mirabelle plums of all hues – dark maroon, amber yellow, red and orange. These make a delicious liqueur/winter warmer as do the bullace plums which are more easily found, so take your choice.

> 5 lbs (2.2kg) sloes, bullace or mirabelle
> plums
> 1 lb (450g) lump sugar
> 1 bottle gin, vodka or brandy

Prick the sloes with a stainless steel or silver fork and put into a clean plastic sweet jar, add the sugar and alcohol of your choice. Cover tightly and leave in a dark cupboard shaking occasionally for the first few weeks to dissolve the sugar. Leave for as long as possible then strain and decant into clean bottles. Add a few drops of almond essence to the sloe gin for variety if you wish. One recipe suggests cracking some of the stones to add the flavour of the kernel to the liqueur, but this is a bit laborious so I don't recommend it.

ARCHIE'S BLOODY MARY

I thought it appropriate that the very last recipe at the end of this book should be Archie's special knock—out drops – in other words the potion he dispenses to his guests after the Tower Hill or 'Ten Acre Shoot'. It appears to be pretty harmless, but is in fact fairly lethal and quite delicious. He usually chooses to make it on the evening before the shoot, just as I am doing some complicated last minute cookery, all of which has to stop as he barks out a list of requirements. The quantity made has to be mixed in a preserving pan and then transferred back into the tomato juice jars and then stowed away in the fridge. But for this recipe I made him scale it down to make enough for 3—4 people. It is much better made the day before to allow the flavours to develop. Taste as you go!

> 1 teaspoon Lemon Pepper   6–8 fl oz (185–225ml) vodka
> 1½ teaspoons oregano   1½ fl oz (45ml) lemon juice
> 2 teaspoons sugar   Worcester Sauce to taste
> 1 x 32.72 fl oz (932ml) jar tomato juice   4 shakes tabasco sauce

Mix the dry ingredients together in a jug, then pour in the tomato juice and stir well. Add the vodka and stir again. Finally add the Worcester Sauce, lemon juice and tabasco and mix well, then pour back into the tomato juice jar and put in the fridge. Lucy likes to add a little dry sherry so when you are serving the Bloody Mary you can pour a little into individual glasses if your guests like it.

Index